CHINESE CURRENCY
CURRENCY
AND GLOBAL
THE GLOBAL
ECONOMY

CHINESE CURRENCY
AND THE GLOBAL ECONOMY

THE RISE OF THE
RENMINBI

CHEN YULU

Mc
Graw
Hill
Education

New York   Chicago   San Francisco   Athens   London
Madrid   Mexico City   Milan   New Delhi
Singapore   Sydney   Toronto

Beijing Jinghua Hucais Printing, Co., Ltd.

ISBN   978-0-07-182990-8
MHID   0-07-182990-3

e-ISBN   978-0-07-182992-2
e-MHID   0-07-182992-X

Library of Congress Cataloging-in-Publication Data
Chen, Yulu.
  Chinese currency and the global economy : the rise of the renminbi / Chen Yulu.
    pages cm
  Includes bibliographical references and index.
  ISBN 978-0-07-182990-8 (hardback)—ISBN 0-07-182990-3 (hardback) 1. Monetary policy—
China. 2. Renminbi. 3. Money—China. I. Title.
  HG1285.C4647 2014.
  332.4'951—dc23   2013029901

McGraw-Hill Education books are available at special quantity discounts to use as premiums and sales promotions or for use in corporate training programs. To contact a representative, please visit the Contact Us pages at www.mhprofessional.com.

CONTENTS

INTRODUCTION   vii

1. THE HISTORICAL EVOLUTION OF CHINA'S
   MONETARY CULTURE   1

2. THE CORNERSTONE OF CHINESE CURRENCY:
   GROWTH WITHOUT CRISIS   25

3. CHINESE MONETARY POLICY   47

4. THE RMB EXCHANGE RATE   75

5. CAPITAL ACCOUNT OPENING IN CHINA   99

6. INTERNATIONAL MONETARY SYSTEM REFORM
   AND RMB GLOBALIZATION   125

NOTES   151
BIBLIOGRAPHY   153
INDEX   157

INTRODUCTION

Since September 2008 a global financial crisis stemming from the American subprime crisis has evolved, spreading from the financial sector to the industrial sector and from the United States to Europe and the rest of the world. The global financial crisis will not only affect the long-term global economy and world finance but also prompt academics and practitioners to analyze the cause and reassess the situation in search of a new mechanism that facilitates sustainable economic development.

The crisis demonstrated that it would be useless to simply patch up the old economic model. A brand-new, sustainable economic mechanism is needed to rescue the world economy before it is too late. It should be universally accessible and benefit world stability. As a future global management model, the new mechanism requires participation and support from growing, developing countries. As a matter of fact, developing economies contributed almost the entire world economic growth in 2009.

As a remarkable developing country, China achieved economic output that accounted for 7.9 percent of total world output and foreign trade volume that amounted to 8 percent of total world volume in 2009. China's foreign exchange reserve has accounted for 28 percent of global foreign exchange reserves. The amount of foreign investment in China has always ranked among the top three in the past decade, and it even ranked number one in some years. With the deepening of its reform and opening up and the acceleration of its modernization, China has closely connected with the world economy, and China's economic growth has been an important engine in global economic stability and recovery.

It should be mentioned that China is now facing the in-depth blend of globalization and modernization, which objectively requires

China to establish a new development pattern that can benefit itself and the world in the extremely complicated international financial environment. On one hand, China has its own unique characteristics, which means China's future development must be carried out according to its national conditions and China will adopt sustainable development with Chinese characteristics. On the other hand, the global issues related to finance are arousing more international concerns. Faced with an increasingly complicated financial environment, China should take a more active and open stance to establish a new worldwide thinking pattern for future economic and financial development.

The so-called global thinking pattern refers to one that is based on mutual interests and development and promotes cross-cultural communication. Since innovative thinking usually takes place with the interaction of different cultures, dynamic balanced management and global creative thinking will help China take a more active role in the rebalancing of the world economy as well as promote the establishment of a global management system based on long-term mutual trust and cooperation.

The harmony of heaven, earth, and human beings is the main trend and strength of traditional Chinese thinking. Hence, in the processes of economic globalization and modernization, effective coordination of the traditional Chinese Doctrine of the Mean, characteristic of integration, intuitive sensibility, reconciliation, and inherent harmony, with Western thinking, which focuses on individuality, independence, deductive reasoning, and the transcendence of external conflicts, will become the core of China's future global thinking pattern. In accordance with these thoughts, China's future economic growth will obtain continuous power from coordination with the global economy. The cooperation of the Chinese currency with the global financial system will lay the foundation for future growth.

It is expected that with a solid economy, stable social structure, and rich culture, China's economic and monetary growth will not only be a reality but also contribute to world economic prosperity and the establishment of a global cooperation model. In view of the above, this book describes China's monetary development against the background of current Chinese conditions and from the global viewpoint to comprehensively and systematically demonstrate the historical background, actual condition, core issues, and ultimate goal of China's monetary development.

This book includes six chapters. Chapter 1 gives a description of the evolutionary path of China's monetary culture from ancient times to today and presents the methodical monetary evolution of China as a large oriental country with thousands of years of civilization. Chapter 2 gives a comprehensive introduction to the history and development of the Chinese economy, which is deemed to be a world miracle, and an in-depth and systematic illustration of its pattern of development without crisis, which is the cornerstone of monetary development. Chapter 3 mainly studies the internal and external environment for the implementation of Chinese monetary policy and the changes to meet economic and financial structural challenges as well as the needs of Chinese monetary development. Chapter 4 comprehensively describes the past, present, and future of the RMB exchange rate and its reform by providing a historical review of the basic RMB exchange rate mechanism and reform of the exchange rate system. Chapter 5 gives a thorough analysis of the basic problems that RMB has to face in order to achieve full convertibility. By taking into account domestic and international conditions, this chapter also forecasts the timing of full convertibility for RMB. Chapter 6 expounds on the historical background and implementation of RMB internationalization and points out that RMB internationalization is an important choice for China in order to participate in the reform of the international monetary system, allowing China to play an important role in global economic growth.

CHAPTER 1

THE HISTORICAL EVOLUTION OF CHINA'S MONETARY CULTURE

From cowries, precious stones and metals, five-zhu copper coins (one zhu equals one twenty-fourth of one tael), and feiqian and jiaozi paper money to present-day Renminbi, the course of evolution in Chinese currency reflects the comprehensive progress in society, politics, economy, and culture in the age-old Chinese civilization. It is a crystallization of the metamorphosis of Chinese culture over the last five thousand years.

Money is the foundation of commerce and economic activity. The monetary system is the fundamental institutional arrangement of socioeconomic interactions. What determines the monetary system is not just the economy, technology, or social system—in a deeper sense, it is predicated on civilization itself. It is civilization that endows money with the magic power to change the world in today's monetary revolution.

Since this chapter refers to numerous periods and dynasties throughout China's history, please feel free to consult Table 1.1 for reference.

Money and Credit in the Pre-Qin and Qin–Han Periods

Chinese culture originated in the vast plains of hinterland China. In the Shang and Zhou dynasties, money in circulation took the form of cowrie shells brought from what are today's Shandong and Maldive

Islands. The Chinese shipped such shells all the way from the sea to central China to meet the needs of princes, marquises, and the nobility for jewelry and ornaments. From the decorative patterns on excavated earthenware dating back to the Shang and the Zhou, it is possible to see people wearing strings of shells on their necks and waists. The nobility were the first to use cowries as a medium of exchange. The face value of this kind of money was based on the value of the jewelry

Table 1.1 The Chronology of Chinese Dynasties

Xia dynasty			about 2070 B.C.–about 1600 BC			Northern Wei	386–534
Shang dynasty			about 1600 BC–about 1046 BC	Northern and Southern dynasties	Northern dynasty	Eastern Wei	534–550
Zhou dynasty	Western Zhou		about 1046 BC–711 BC			Northern Qi	550–577
	Eastern Zhou		770 BC–256 BC			Western Wei	535–557
	Spring and Autumn Period		770 BC–476 BC			Northern Zhou	557–581
	Warring States Period		475 BC–221 BC		Sui dynasty		581–618
Qin dynasty			221 BC–206 BC		Tang dynasty		618–907
Han dynasty	Western Han		206 BC–9 AD	Five Dynasties and Ten Kingdoms	Later Liang		907–923
	Xin		9–24		Later Tang		923–936
	Eastern Han		25–220		Later Jin		936–946
The Three Kingdoms	Wei state		220–265		Later Han		947–950
	Shu state		221–263		Later Zhou		951–960
	Wu state		222–280		Ten Kingdoms		902–979
Eastern Jin dynasty Sixteen Kingdoms	Western Jin		265–316	Song dynasty	Northern Song		960–1127
	Eastern Jin		317–420		Southern Song		1127–1279
	Sixteen Kingdoms		304–439		Liao		907–1125
Northern and Southern dynasties	Southern dynasty	Song	420–479		Western Xia		1038–1227
		Qi	479–502		Jin dynasty		1115–1234
		Liang	502–557		Yuan dynasty		1279–1368
		Chen	557–589		Ming dynasty		1368–1644
Note: The Ten Kingdoms include Former Shu, Later Shu, Wuyue, Min, Chu, Wu, Jingnan (Nanping), Southern Han, Northern Han, and Southern Tang.					Qing dynasty		1644–1911
					The Republic of China		1912–1949

they were wearing. One string of 10 cowries equaled one *peng* and 20 *peng* were worth three *mu* of farmland. People were accustomed to using cowries as legal tender through long years of trading activities. In this way, the cowrie shell became the progenitor of the Chinese currency.

With productivity growing steadily, dukedoms of the Spring and Autumn Period began to build post roads to facilitate communication and transportation. As transportation became more and more convenient, cowrie shells were no longer a rarity and therefore lost their function as a measure of value. With the invention of metal smelting technology during that period, bronze, gold, and silver replaced cowries to become major raw coinage materials. At the time, people were yet to be awakened to the concept of credit, and the circulation of money was based on the money's utility value. In ancient times, money in circulation was not issued by the government, which means there was no difference between good money and bad money. Copper coins were fashioned in the shape of their predecessors—cowrie shells—for everyday use, hence the term "copper shells." Cake-sized copper coins, or "copper cakes," came in handy when bulk commodities changed hands. Both copper shells and copper cakes may be called "money measured by weight," which, like cowrie shells, were born of economic development. After the Spring and Autumn Period, copper became the main raw material for coinage.

In the Spring and Autumn and the Warring States Periods, differences between dukedoms of the Zhou dynasty in economic development, productivity, and folkways gave rise to diverse forms of money. The Chinese currency embarked on a road of diversified development as a result. The money circulated in every dukedom bore distinctive features of the local mode of production and lifestyle, leaving clues about the course along which the Chinese civilization evolved. The money in circulation in those years fell into three general categories: first, spade-shaped coins circulating in the central Chinese dukedom of Jin that later split into three states—Zhao, Han, and Wei; second, knife-shaped money in the coastal states of Qi and Lu; and third, the shell-shaped copper coins in the state of Chu in present-day Hubei Province, with the city of Jingzhou at its center.

The dukedom of Jin, carved into three pieces by the dukes of Han, Wei, and Zhao in 359 BC, was situated in the middle reaches of the Yellow River and the Guanlong and Heluo areas. As agriculture was already a dominant tradition in that part of China in those years, the coins in circulation there took the shape of a *bo*, a spadelike farm tool used to hoe up weeds. Obviously, the spade shape of the coins symbolized the local people's dream for a reposed farming life and reflected the everyday life of farmers who began tilling the land at sunrise and went home at sunset on the Loess Plateau. The land of Jin was the cradle of the Legalist school of thought, as its leaders—Han Fei (281–233 BC), Shen Buhai (385–337 BC), and Shang Yang (395–338 BC)—were born there. That is probably why many spade-shaped coins in that region bore the pictographic character *tian* 田, a symbol of the stringent statecraft advocated by the Legalists.

Different from the vast hinterland China, the land of coastal eastern China that was home to the states of Qi and Lu was unfriendly to farming. According to the *Records of the Great Historian*, the territory of Qi was where "the sea dumped its salt, turning it into saline-alkali land that kept the yield of the five cereals low and left local people in poverty." However, the people of Qi and Lu, "honing their skills to excellence and becoming adept in dealing in fish and salt," launched booming fishery and weaving-and-spinning undertakings. Industry and commerce thrived as a result. Six of the state of Qi's 21 townships were industrial and commercial centers where "hats, belts, clothes, and shoes made in the state of Qi were sold all over the country, while one duke after another arrived from the East Sea and Mount Taishan to pay homage to Qi in hushed awe and reverence."

Most coins in circulation in Qi assumed the shape of a knife, denoting not a weapon but a fishing tool popular with local fishermen. In keeping with the reputation of the Qi and Lu as the cradle of Confucianism, the design of this knife features a concave back and a convex blade that combine to look round outwardly and square inwardly. The wisdom of Confucius's countrymen was best exemplified in the exquisiteness of this knife-shaped coin—its length of 18 centimeters is equivalent to that of a human hand, and six such coins can be put together to form a perfect circle.

In contrast to hinterland China, the state of Chu in the Yangtze River valley belonged in the southern branch of Chinese civilization. Its land in Hubei Province, with Jingzhou at the center, was an expanse of hills and marshes unsuitable for grain and cotton crops. The ancestors of the local people overcame these natural adversities and developed a powerful handicraft industry. The best lacquerware from China at the time was made in the state of Chu, and as archeological discoveries indicate, these products were sold all the way to southeast and central Asia. During the Spring and Autumn and Warring States Periods, commerce in the Jingzhou area was probably the most developed in China. As the birthplace of Taoism, that area was also known for its splendid and somewhat mysterious culture. While people in the central plains worshipped heaven, folks of Jingzhou believed in witchcraft and wizardry. Their metal money, a kind of "copper shell," resembles a cowrie shell. As the local mountains abounded in gold ore, the state of Chu was the leading gold producer in China. The gold from that state spread to other parts of the country alongside shiploads of lacquerware on the Yangtze River. Hence the old refrain, "Gold comes from the state of Chu."

Gold had already become an important currency by the Spring and Autumn and Warring States Periods. To cite the *Records of the Great Historian* again, "After Su Qin talked the king of Zhao into forming a coalition of six states, the king rewarded him with a hundred chariots and a thousand *yi* of gold" (1 *yi* equals 20 *taels*).

The shape of this kind of money remains unknown to this day, but one thing is certain: gold was already a precious currency by weight at the time. "Gold money weighed by *yuan*," cast in the state of Chu, and in the Chu capital city of Ying in particular, was a major form of money. *Yuan* was a measuring unit for money by weight.

During the Warring States Period, Ying Zheng, the king of Qin, conquered the rivaling states of Han in 230 BC, Zhao in 228 BC, Wei in 225 BC, Chu in 223 BC, and Yan in 222 BC. In 221 BC, he eventually eliminated the Qi and unified China in a feudal monarchy. Since then China has been able to overcome incessant domestic scrambles between warlords and invasions by alien powers to remain a unified nation with Han people composing the majority of the population.

After establishing the Qin dynasty, which was China's first feudal empire, the first emperor proclaimed, "Gold, to be measured under the *yi* weighing system, is to be the upper currency; a coin of bronze that has a fixed weight of half a tael, with its denomination matching its true value, shall serve as the lower currency; pearls, jade, tortoise shells, and cowries, as well as silver and tin fall into the category of jewelry, ornaments, and collectables—they are not to be used as money." During his short-lived reign, Hu Hai, the second emperor of the Qin dynasty, issued one edict after another to demand establishing the half-tael bronze coins as the official currency, a fact that indicates his failure to execute the monetary system initiated by Ying Zheng. The half-tael coins never became the standard currency even after the Qin dynasty met its demise at the hands of peasant rebels.

After the Qin dynasty gave way to Liu Bang's Western Han dynasty, illegal minting of coins ran rampant under the protection of the newly enfeoffed, powerful dukes. It remained a serious problem even after Liu Bang issued an edict to sanction it. Whether by repeatedly changing the weighing system for the official coinage or by replacing eight-zhu coins with three-zhu ones in its early days, the Western Han dynasty was not able to unify its monetary system. At its wit's end, the government had no alternative but to permit dukes to cast their own coins under the pretext of "letting citizens cast money." That action was of little use, as the unification of a currency calls for a developed economy and an all-powerful central authority.

It was not until the reign of Liu Che, the Emperor Wu of Han, that the coinage system was unified. According to the new government stipulation that "all the copper delivered to the state should not be minted into coins" and that "those guilty of piratical coinage shall, without exception, be sentenced to death," those who illegally cast money were subject to stern punishment.

Liu Che worked to promote three-zhu coins and platinum coins. But both efforts failed—disparity between the real value of both types of coins and their denominations had spawned problems in their circulation. Eventually the emperor changed his mind, deciding to put five-zhu coins in circulation.

The five-zhu coin was a major breakthrough in China's monetary history. The government eventually found a feasible value for the currency among all sorts of money by weight. Moreover, the emperor was also able to monopolize copper production and reserves. Both factors explain why the five-zhu coin could become a stable currency in the latter part of Liu Che's reign. In spite of the regent Wang Mang's attempt to change the monetary system in the twilight years of the Western Han dynasty, the prestige of the five-zhu coin stayed untarnished. The public continued to trust it during Wang Mang's rule, which was best described in this folk rhyme: "A yellow-skinned ox ought to have a white belly; the five-zhu coin deserves to be brought back."

Large-scale credit was already in existence during the Han dynasty. One kind of credit was given by the government for the relief of victims of famine and natural disasters. Although there were records about this form of credit prior to the Han dynasty, they were not elaborate enough to make sense. The *Book of Han* gives a relatively clear record. According to it, the largest scale of governmental credit happened in 120 BC after Shandong was inundated by floods. Since it would take years for the land to regain fertility after the disaster and the cost of long-term relief was high, Liu Che evacuated 700,000 flood victims to Kuaiji, where their food and clothes were supplied free of charge and their production tools were provided by the government on credit.

The second kind of credit was nongovernmental. The lender was known as "*ziqian* holder" and the money to be lent was *ziqian*, meaning "money that can make more money." As far as historical records go, the largest-scale nongovernmental borrowing in the history of the Han dynasty took place during a rebellion of seven princes. During that period, Liu Qi, the Emperor Jing of Han, collected funds from dukes, princes, and citizens to fight the rebelling princes. A family surnamed "Wuyan" in Chang'an lent a thousand taels of gold to the royal army. After the rebellion was quelled, the repayment the family received was 10 times more than what it had lent. In one year's time, the family of Wuyan became the richest in the Central Shaanxi Plain.

Lending by monks and temples was the third kind of credit. During the Han dynasty, Buddhist monasteries had begun to give credit to local residents and princes and aristocrats. With Buddhism steadily gaining ground in the Northern and Southern dynasties, monks and monasteries became powerful enough to lend money for the relief of disaster victims.

Money and Credit in the Sui and Tang Dynasties and the Song and Yuan Periods

In AD 518 Yang Jian, a North Zhou dynasty minister, dethroned the dynasty's last emperor and proclaimed himself Emperor Wen. Although the Sui dynasty he founded was short-lived, as it went through only two emperors in 38 years, it was a watershed period in Chinese monetary history. It is safe to say it was not until the Sui dynasty that the Chinese currency was really unified for the first time in history. Although Ying Zheng, the first emperor of the Qin dynasty, had tried to unify the money, the feudal system he had personally founded did a poor job in executing his order. Emperor Wen coined the five-zhu money again, known in history as the "five-zhu money of the Sui." When the five-zhu coins of the Sui were issued, outdated currencies were still in circulation. The emperor issued the order that "all the old money used in the marketplace shall be confiscated by the government" and cracked down on those who illegally minted coins.

Chinese feudalism reached a pinnacle during the Tang dynasty. That is why many overseas Chinese today still proudly call themselves "Tang people." The Tang dynasty was the most brilliant era in ancient China, and its influence on China and the world is still keenly felt to this day. In the heyday of the Tang dynasty, China's grain output per capita amounted to 4,524 *jin*, a record that stayed unsurpassed as late as 1978, when the figure was a meager 2,214 *jin*. When Li Shimin, the Emperor Taizhong, started his reign of Zhenguan, he issued kaiyuan tongbao, the "coin to inaugurate the reign." This coin was first cast by his father, Li Yuan, in 621 or the fourth year of the reign of Wude, but historians generally regarded it as a symbol of the prosperous reign of Zhenguan. Kaiyuan tongbao was not measured by weight, with 10 such coins equaling one tael (37.5 grams) or 10 qian, and it put an end to the circulation of the five-zhu coins dating back to the Western Han dynasty. Since then the Chinese currency has never been based on weight. However, with development in production and growth in the volume of everyday transactions, kaiyuan tongbao showed its limits, for it was designed for use mainly among landholding peasants. Merchants and government officials gradually used gold and silver to handle large payments and transactions. However, gold and silver never became a popular medium of exchange during the Tang dynasty.

A lack of coins in circulation was the number one headache during the early years of the Tang dynasty. The weight of *kaiyuan tongbao* was never reduced. Its minting cost, averaging 900 coins for every *guan* or string of 1,000 coins, was boosted as a result of maladministration, while the supply of coins in circulation was always short of demand. As a result, illegal coinage prevailed once again. Illegal coins in circulation could have led to a price hike, but prices were surprisingly stable during the early Tang dynasty. The reason behind it was that under the reign of Emperor Li Shimin, production was developed to a point where the sum total of governmental and illegal coins was not large enough to meet the demand for money in circulation, so much so that the dynasty had to resort to deflation to keep the economy going in its early period.

By the middle of the 685–762 reign of Li Longji, the Emperor Xuanzong, grain prices in the capital city of Chang'an dropped to 15 *qian* per *dan* (1 *dan* equals approximately 1 hectoliter). This prompted Chancellor Zhang Jiuling (678–740) to record what happened in the monetary system in his book *On Coins*. In that book, he advocated decontrolling private coinage and enunciated the following theory on the quantity of money supply: In comparison with primitive barter trade, exchange through money is progress, but because the government has failed to profit from its mints, the quantity of the coin supply is bound to shrink, which will bring market prices down as a result. Reduced market prices tend to cut the grain price to the detriment of the immediate interests of peasants. His solution to the problem was to allow private citizens to cast their own money. Under Zhang Jiuling's maneuvering, individuals were given a free hand to mint coins, and the increased output greatly alleviated the strain on the money supply.

The growing commodities economy gave rise to diverse forms of credit such as *feiqian* or "money on the fly," money shops for the safe-keeping of money, and government-run usury during the middle and late periods of the Tang dynasty. To cope with money-supply short-ages, many localities banned the export of copper coins during the Tang dynasty. That was why the Chinese began to make use of *feiqian*, a kind of money order for remittance and cashing purposes.

As with every dynasty in Chinese history, provinces, prefectures, and counties were obliged to pay taxes to the central government. In the early Tang dynasty, they had to pay taxes by delivering coins directly to Chang'an; after the mid-Tang, more and more merchants operating in the capital city shipped the money they had made in the capital city all the way back home. The transfer of coins to and fro increased costs; it was also prone to safety problems. To cope with the situation, various circuits (a provincial-level administrative division) set up "memorial submission offices" in Chang'an where merchants went to deliver their money in return for a certificate and had a copy of it mailed to a local office, so that a merchant could go home to have the certificate cashed. At the same time, the memorial submission offices could ship the coins collected from the merchants to the state treasury as tax payments. The certificate was aptly termed *feiqian*, the money on the fly; it was not paper money, but a kind of money order designed for remittance and cashing purposes.

The burgeoning commerce of the Tang dynasty also gave birth to the first generation of savings agencies—the money shop. Prior to the Tang dynasty, big merchants had to bring money and cash surpluses along with them, or deposit their money in inns or in their relatives' or friends' homes. Money shops emerged during the Tang dynasty for the single purpose of receiving savings deposits from merchants and local residents. These money shops originated from the cabinets provided by inns. With a permit issued by an innkeeper, a traveler could keep his money in such a cabinet, and open or close it with his own lock and key. In his absence, his friends could also come to fetch the money with the key after showing the permit to the innkeeper. There was no fixed pattern for the permit—the authenticity of it hinged on the innkeeper's memory. By the middle and late Tang, the money shops began to accept savings deposits, where merchants could also take out a mortgage on their goods. Tales about the money shops were mostly found in novels. Such tales may be fictional, but they shed precious light on what really happened in those years.

In the Sui and Tang dynasties the best-known and most controversial governmental credit was "yeomen money"—a kind of government-run usury started from the Sui. Managers of this usury were known as "money-snatching officials." When the first two Tang emperors, Li Yuan and Li Shimin, followed the example of the Sui dynasty and instituted the position of "money-snatching historians," their intention was to provide jobs for superfluous officials. The task of a money-snatching official was to use government revenue as principal to issue usurious loans to residents and to rely on government force to recover the principal and interest. This practice was riddled with malpractices, as some officials abused their power to line their own pockets by lending money at a high interest rate and recovering the principal and interest through government channels. The revenue from the yeomen money was at the disposal of local officials who also profited by running usury as a sideline occupation. The government background and money-lending behavior of the money-snatching officials thus became a source of public doubt and scorn. The practice of yeomen money continued off and on during the Sui and the Tang, but it was never really terminated.

Many emperors of the Song dynasty were fond of inscribing coins in their own handwriting. The "currency of the Chongning Reign" and the "currency of the Daguan Reign," wrought by Zhao Ji or Emperor Huizong in vigorous and flourishing strokes that were a trademark of his thin-stroked calligraphy, are regarded as exquisite objects of art. China developed the world's most advanced commodities economy during the Song dynasty, and the best known of that dynasty's currency was not copper coins but *jiaozi*, meaning "voucher for exchange," the first paper money in human history.

During the Song dynasty, commerce had developed to a point where copper coins could no longer meet the circulation demand. During the Jingde reign of Emperor Zhenzong, the people of what is present-day Chengdu, where economic prosperity was second only to that of the two Zhejiang circuits, invented *jiaozi* to make up for shortages in the supply of cast coins in circulation. According to the *Book of Song*, this kind of money order appeared toward the end of the tenth century. In the beginning, 16 rich local merchants monopolized the circulation of jiaozi under a jointly guaranteed cash-and-pay framework. With these 16 merchants, whose names were confidential, invested with the decoding power, the first generation of jiaozi coded to prevent fraud became a nationwide legal tender. The first batch of government-issued paper money was issued in the inaugural year of the Tiansheng reign by the Chengdu government and in the fourth year of the Ningxi reign by the central government. Though such money was ostensibly for nationwide circulation, it was popular only in Shaanxi, hence its name, "Shaanxi jiaozi." The fame of the Northern Song jiaozi stemmed from the fact that it was the earliest paper money in the world. However, issued by either rich merchants or the government, with no true reserves behind it under most circumstances, jiaozi could be circulated only within a few designated regions.

What was in widest national circulation during the Song dynasty was not jiaozi but a kind of negotiable paper for salt transactions. More popular than jiaozi in terms of scope, duration, and amount in circulation, such negotiable paper was also known as a "paying voucher" issued by taxation and revenue authorities. During the Song dynasty, after a merchant had paid for government-monopolized salt, iron, tea, or other goods, he would obtain such a voucher with which to get the goods he had paid for. This kind of negotiable paper, which had the same effect as cast coins, already became an exchange medium in the early Northern Song dynasty. It was a de facto, officially endorsed currency. Different from jiaozi, the circulation of this negotiable paper was guaranteed with a real commodity—salt. The emperors of the Song dynasty, however, kept a tight rein on its circulation, while their ranking officials, including Wang Anshi, Pi Gongbi, and Cai Jing, had worked to restrict its circulation.

The Chinese economy was well developed by the Southern Song dynasty. The capital city of Lin'an, which is today's Hangzhou, was a natural transportation hub, as it was situated on the northern bank of the Qiantang River and the southern end of the Grand Canal, with the picturesque West Lake nestled in the city proper. In its heyday, Hangzhou's population topped 1.2 million, and the city had 414 commercial entities that were clustered along its streets according to trades and professions.

People may wonder why the well-developed economy of the Southern Song dynasty did not give rise to its own gold or silver standard. Gold and silver can become currency only when their value is in equilibrium with that of the commodities in circulation. During the Song dynasty, China's smelting technology was at about the same level as Western Europe, but its agriculture and handicrafts were far better developed. Thus the value of goods in circulation in China had outgrown the carrying capacity of gold and silver. As the supply of gold and silver could not keep pace with the booming economy, they never became major coinage materials. That is why during the Tang and Song dynasties, gold and silver were merely used by the rich and powerful to amass wealth or to bribe the government for exemptions. According to early Tang records, a man could pay 14 taels of silver in return for exemption from a year's forced labor, a price that no small-time peasant families could afford.

In 1297 the Mongols toppled the Southern Song, and the Yuan dynasty moved to central China and unified the country again, but its reign was short-lived. The Yuan dynasty carried forward its tradition of using silver as its currency. That was why the silver ingots in circulation were called *yuanbao*, "the treasure of Yuan."

When Kublai Khan (1215–1294) proclaimed himself the founding emperor of Yuan in 1271, he followed the Jin dynasty's example to issue the "Zhongtong-reign Currency," which could be converted into gold and silver from the government treasury. It was the first paper money in Chinese history based on the gold and silver standards. In 1263 the Khan set up a buffer-fund treasury to regulate the exchange rates between the Zhongtong-reign currency and gold and silver. This treasury, whose function was akin to that of a present-day central bank, did a good job in implementing the government monetary policy. The *Book of Yuan* recorded no inflation prior to 1275, but the paper money of the Zhongtong reign not only was in circulation in the vast territory of the Yuan dynasty but also found its way to Europe.

During the Northern Song dynasty, military power was designated to the Privy Council, whereby soldiers and generals belonged to different commands, so that soldiers knew little about their commanders and vice versa. This military establishment rendered the dynasty ineffective in dealing with invasions by the swift northern nomads from the Liao and Jin dynasties. The rulers had no choice but to keep peace by paying an annual pacification tribute to these nomads. Such annual payments eventually became a heavy financial burden on the Northern Song government, so much so that the dynasty was already tottering in turmoil less than a century after Zhao Kuangyin (927–976) founded the dynasty.

To deliver the dynasty from the crisis, Wang Anshi (1021–1086) submitted a 10,000-word petition for reform to Zhao Zhen, Emperor Renzong, in 1058, the third year of the Jiayou reign. In the petition Wang said, "It is to the benefit of the entire nation for wealth to be produced throughout the country, and in the same token, wealth should be obtained from across the country to cover the expenses of the entire nation." In 1068, or the first year of the Ningxi reign, Zhao Xu, Emperor Shenzong, issued an edict to Wang Anshi to commence what is known in Chinese history as Wang Anshi's Reform.

Wang's reform was centered on two forms of government credit, the "green seedling act" and the "market transaction law."

The green seedling act was none other than government loans at a 40 percent interest rate, to be extended to peasants during the time of the year when crops were still in the blade while the granary was nearly exhausted. The principal and interest were to be repaid after the next harvest season was over, with the interest collected and put at the disposal of local governments. During the Northern Song period, rural China was under a *bao-jia* administrative system whereby households were grouped into *bao* and *jia*, with each jia consisting of 10 households and each *bao* comprising 10 *jia*. The repayment of the green seedling loans was guaranteed collectively by every *bao*, so that when one household failed to repay such a loan, it was the responsibility of all the households in a *bao* to repay it.

The market transaction law stipulated that for every million strings of 1,000 cash deposited in the state treasury, 870,000 strings were to be used as capital to control market prices. In the same fashion as the green seedling act, this law allowed the government to issue loans to merchants at a 20 percent annual interest rate.

Wang Anshi's reform met with stubborn opposition from within and without the government. The chief opponent was Prime Minister Sima Guang, who asserted, "The multitude of wealth and goods born of heaven and earth was limited—they were in the possession of either civilians or the government." According to him, now that nongovernmental usury could rob people of their land and leave them in hunger, cold, and homelessness, government-mandated usury could do worse—it was meant to exploit and dispossess the small-time peasants, with the ultimate result that "the wealth of rich families is to be drained, the order of society upset, and the state treasury emptied."

Wang Anshi's reform improved the central government's balance of payments but at the same time committed mistakes when the reform measures were implemented in many places. By contrast, Sima Guang's idea smacked of modern-day Western monetarism, which is opposed to excessive government intervention in economic affairs. As is the case with the disputes between Keynesian economics and monetarism, both Wang Anshi and Sima Guang deserve our respect, because their ideas, though not 100 percent correct, helped boost the economy to a certain extent.

Money and Credit in the
Ming and Qing Dynasties

When Zhu Yuanzhang established the Ming dynasty in 1368, he immediately issued the copper coins known as the "currency of the Hongwu Reign." The public, however, blamed the government for "making too much ado" about the new currency, for by that time the value of copper coins could no longer meet the demand of everyday transactions, while silver had begun to gain popularity among nongovernmental traders. In the new dynasty's early period, the remnant of Yuan influence was still going strong in the north, making shipments of copper coins and silver ingots from the capital city of Nanjing in the south both unsafe and inconvenient. The government coped with the situation by issuing the "paper money of the Great Ming" based on the silver standard.

This silver-based paper money initiated by Zhu Yuanzhang was inherited by his successors, Zhu Yunwen (Emperor Jianwen) and Zhu Di (Emperor Mingcheng). Thus a currency based on precious metals money went onstage in Chinese monetary history. During the mid-Ming dynasty, Prime Minister Zhang Juzheng (1525–1582) streamlined the taxation system with his "single whip method." One of the steps he took was to abolish corvee (required public labor) and replace it with tax levies in silver. This greatly stimulated the commodities economy of the Ming dynasty, put an end to the farming and weaving lifestyle of the self-sufficient landowning peasants who formed the foundation of the dynasty's taxation system, and forced them to sell their products on the market. Silver also catalyzed the development of the handicraft industry. The embryo of capitalism was already emerging by the mid-Ming dynasty.

In the late Jin dynasty (1616–1644), the Manchurians used silver ingots as money. That explains why the *Records of Emperor Taizong of the Qing* provide no records about paper money or copper coins. The only paper money issued in the early Qing history, after Emperor Shunzhi moved south of the Great Wall and ascended the throne in Beijing, was known as "stringed money," but no samples of it are extant today. In 1646, or the third year of his reign, the emperor straightened out the circulation of silver, and the official currency earned a good reputation.

Emperor Shunzhi outlawed the use of silver of low purity and make-believe silver made of an alloy of silver, tin, and lead, and recast the silver that had been collected as a tax in kind to produce what are known as the "big silver ingots" with a 93 percent purity. In 1681, or the twenty-third year of his reign, Emperor Kangxi lifted the government ban on maritime trade. China's peculiar small-peasant economy, plus the fact that the Chinese were yet to be accustomed to daily necessities from the West, enabled the Qing dynasty to maintain a favorable balance of trade for a long time. Foreign silver dollars, most of which were Spanish coins cast in Mexico with wheat-ear patterns on their edges, became not uncommon in China's coastal cities. The arrival of foreign currencies enriched the Chinese currency with such denominating units as *kuai* and *yuan*.

Money shops, indigenous Chinese monetary organizations appearing in the early Ming dynasty and flourishing during the mid-Qing dynasty, had their roots in ordinary stores where people went shopping while having their silver fragments recast into coins. Those stores that enjoyed a good reputation in silver recasting gradually earned the respect of shoppers, who called them "money shops." Descriptions of such shops are found often in such Ming dynasty novels as Feng Menglong's *Stories Old and New: A Ming Dynasty Collection*. More stories about the money shops appeared in fiction in the late reign of Emperor Qianlong, but their function had changed—they had stopped retail sales to concentrate on converting silver dollars into copper coins.

By the reign of Emperor Jiaqing, the business line of these shops had extended to loans. On the eve of the Opium War of 1840, money shop chains emerged, and remittance and cashing services between destinations became available.

Exchange shops, another Chinese invention, were born of expanded commodities circulation during the Ming–Qing interregnum. The first exchange shop was founded by Lei Lutai, owner of the Xiyu Dye Stuff Shop headquartered in Pingyao County, Shanxi, and with branches in Beijing, Shenyang, and Sichuan. As his business reached a sizable scale, Lei's shop and branches began remitting money and cashing money orders for business partners. In 1823, the third year of the Daoguang reign, the Xiyu Dye Stuff Shop was renamed Rishengchang Exchange Shop to deal exclusively in remittance and cashing services. Prior to the Opium War of 1840, there were only seven exchange shops in Shanxi. The best known of them was the Five-Shop Chain of Pingyao, where funds were dispatched and regulated between these shops in support of their money-changing services.

An exchange shop was generally owned by an investor and operated by a manager, with local celebrities invited to proof its volume of capital or clarify its shares if it was run on a shareholding basis. In the meantime, a special account was opened so that clerks could become shareholders by their participation. In a system that separated ownership and management, the daily operation of an exchange shop was the responsibility of the shop manager, while the task of the shop owner was to supervise the accounts toward the end of a year.

The exchange shops of Shanxi province were known for their strict management. Their well-defined secret coding system, their system whereby branches were required to report to the headquarters at regular intervals, and the headquarters' monopoly of the billing right, with branches banned from printing their own bills of exchange, are still being highly acclaimed today. Trade between south and north China, and remittance and cashing services were vital to the destiny of these exchange shops. After Hong Xiuquan (1814–1864) founded the Heavenly Kingdom (1851–1864), the Qing dynasty lost control of the region south of the Yangtze River, and local exchange shops run by Shanxi merchants were evacuated as a result. But the civil war had little adverse effect on the growth of Shanxi's exchange shops. As it happened, during the war the Qing government was still in need of a money flow between north and south, as local tax payments had to be shipped to the capital city while the central government cash provisions had to be shipped to localities.

In 1862, or the first year of the Tongzhi reign, the warring prompted the Ministry of Revenue to order viceroys and provincial governors across the country to "find well-established private banking

houses to remit and cash provisions from the central government."
In 1865 the delivery of local cash tax payments to the central government was replaced with remittance and cashing operations. Those
Shanxi exchange shops that were commissioned to provide such services obtained a whopping sum of floating capital and began to do
what the central bank and central financial department of today are
supposed to do. Their reputation was greatly boosted as well.

The Birth and Development of Renminbi

In the early years of the Republic of China, the national territory
fell apart between rivaling warlords, and the monetary system was
in disarray. The republican government established a gold transaction standard as the standard for its new currency, unified the
weight and purity of copper coins, and notified governors of various provinces that "in order to maintain the monetary system, the
power of issuing banknotes belongs to the central government." However, the wanton issuance of military currency by the Republic's ill-
prepared Nanjing government led by Provisional President Sun Yat-
sen speeded up its downfall. As a result, the political power was
usurped by Yuan Shikai.

Yuan Shikai shared Sun Yat-sen's dream for a unified currency. In
1912, the "currency reform committee" he had masterminded put forward three reform proposals: first, to institute the gold exchange standard; second, to implement the double gold and silver standards; and
third, to practice the silver standard. In compliance with the Stipula-
tions on the National Currency, the state settled on the silver standard.
Accordingly a new coin, which weighed seven *qian* and two *fens* and
consisted of 90 percent silver and 10 percent copper, was minted. As
it bore a head portrait of Yuan Shikai, the coin was aptly nicknamed
"Big-headed Yuan."

As a matter of fact, the Republic government under the control of
northern warlords never succeeded in unifying the nation's monetary
system. The disorganized monetary system was somewhat rectified
briefly under the rule of Yuan Shikai but went back to chaos shortly

afterward. The market at the time was filled with all descriptions of money: silver fragments, ingots, and coins; copper dollars; banknotes from various foreign countries or issued by the Central Bank and the Bank of Communications; paper money printed by the central government, small Chinese banks, and local banks; and so forth.

In 1927 the renowned economist Ma Yinchu called for unifying the national currency. A national economic conference held in 1928 endorsed a plan to replace the tael with the dollar, but the plan was not executed until 1933. The major obstacle came from money shops that controlled the *yangli*, or exchange rate between the tael and the dollar, and thereby monopolized the money exchange in the marketplace. In March 1933 Shanghai, already the nation's monetary center, was the first to abolish the tael and institute the dollar, and it disbanded the exchange-rate market. As the replacement went smoothly in Shanghai, other regions soon followed suit. After the national government announced the plan in July 1933, the replacement of the tael with the dollar acquired the legal backing it needed. Thereafter, the Bank of China, the Central Bank, and the Bank of Communications (with the addition of the China Peasants' Bank in 1935) were invested with the power to issue the *fabi*, the nation's legal tender or fiat money.

After the War of Resistance against Japan broke out in 1937, the Chinese government adopted a foreign exchange control policy. The *fabi* became the standard paper currency, and a deadline was set to withdraw other paper currencies from circulation. In the initial stage, the Chinese legal tender was pegged to the British pound sterling and could be converted liberally in designated banks. In 1936, the national government reached an agreement with the United States to sell silver to America, with the money earned in U.S. dollars serving as foreign exchange reserves for the circulation of fabi. Thus the Chinese legal tender was pegged to both the pound and the dollar. On August 19, 1948, the fabi was replaced by the gold yuan banknote. The latter came into circulation in August 1948 but was withdrawn nine months later in May 1949.

On November 18, 1948, the North China People's Government convened an administrative conference to deliberate, among other things, how to unify the nation's currency. At the time, the liberated areas were filled with all descriptions of money. Apart from the banknotes issued by the Shanxi-Chahar-Hebei Border, the South Hebei Border Area, the Beihai Bank, the Northwestern Peasants' Bank, the Northeastern Bank, and the Great Wall Bank, there were also fabi, gold yuan banknotes, and silver yuan banknotes issued by the Kuomintang government.

In the same month, the North China People's Government issued a public notice: "To meet the needs of national economic construction, we have reached a consensus with the governments of Shandong province, the Shaanxi-Gansu-Ningxia Border Area, and the Shanxi-Suiyuan Border Areas to adopt a unified currency for circulation in north China, northeast China and northwest China." On December 1, 1948, the North China Bank, the Beihai Bank, and the Northwestern Peasants' Bank were merged to form the People's Bank of China. At nine o'clock that day, the People's Bank of China delivered the first batch of Renminbi banknotes to the Pingshan County Bank. Thus the standard currency of New China was born. The Renminbi, printed on a kind of paper with cotton as the principal raw material, does not contain a specified gold content; it is backed by government tax revenues and state-owned commodities and materials. Therefore, the Chinese currency is totally disassociated from gold. The introduction of Renminbi put an end to a century of chaos in the Chinese monetary system, safeguarded the integrity and unity of the Chinese sovereignty on its legal tender, and ushered the nation into a new period of historical development characterized by a stable currency and a burgeoning economy.

The People's Bank of China is the leading authority for the administration of Renminbi. It is responsible for the design, printing, and issuance of Chinese currency. Since its establishment on December 1, 1948, this bank has issued five series of Renminbi and developed a currency system that includes banknotes, coins, and commemorative coins fashioned out of both ordinary and precious metals.

The Five Series of Renminbi

- The first series of Renminbi, in circulation from December 1, 1948, to December 1953;
- The second series of Renminbi, in circulation from March 1, 1953, to April 20, 1962;
- The third series of Renminbi, in circulation from April 20, 1962, to January 5, 1974;
- The fourth series of Renminbi, in circulation from April 27, 1987, to September 22, 1998;
- The fifth series of Renminbi, which has been in circulation since October 1, 1999.

The unit of Renminbi is the *yuan*, and its fractional units are the *jiao* and the *fen*. The mutual matrixing relations between these units are as follows: 1 yuan equals 10 jiao, and 1 jiao equals 10 fen. Renminbi is abbreviated as CNY in the ISO 4217 system, but the abbreviation RMB is more popular around the world. The volume of Renminbi is generally expressed by putting the sign ¥ (derived from the capital first letter of the word *yuan*) in front of a relevant statistic. At present, with the exception of coins of 1 fen, 2 fen, and 5 fen, the first, second, and third series of Renminbi have been withdrawn from circulation, with the fifth and fourth series in current circulation. The RMB banknotes currently in circulation bear the following denominations: 1 jiao, 2 jiao, 5 jiao, 1 yuan, 2 yuan, 5 yuan, 10 yuan, 20 yuan, 50 yuan, and 100 yuan. The RMB coins feature such denominations as 1 fen, 2 fen, 5 fen, 1 jiao, 5 jiao, and 1 yuan.

Demarcation Between World Civilizations and Evolution of Chinese Money

There are numerous records about the origin of the Chinese currency. The grand historian Sima Qian pointed out, "In the eras of Yu and Xia, the gold used as money came in three grades." According to him, the origin of money "dates back to remote antiquity—it was already in existence as early as before the era of Gaoxin (the sobriquet of Emperor Ku), even though there is no written record about it." Sang Hongyang (152–80 BC) had this to say: "Money changes with the times. The use of dyed-black cowries as money began after the Xia dynasty. The people of the Zhou dynasty used purple stone as a medium of exchange. Cowries and metal coins came in use in a later period." Ye Shi (1150–1223) of the Song dynasty said, "The currency stemmed from merchants on business trips, when exchanges between people from different quarters became well developed." A wealth of written records indicate that China was a forerunner in world monetary history. The credit form of the Chinese money with its distinctly oriental characteristics figures prominently among all currencies in the world, and the demarcation between civilizations bears its ingrained mark.

People tend to believe that the first market appeared in the West, while the Eastern nation of China has been known for its small-time agrarian economy since ancient times. In fact, a peasant household in feudal China could not survive on its own despite the presence of cities with more than one million residents each. These feudal cities accommodated social and industrial divisions of labor and depended upon innovation to overcome obstacles to economic growth. For the survival of their race, the Chinese chose to counter foreign enemies and nature with collective strength, for, in ancient times when people had to grapple with nature using sheer muscle, the strength of a collective was obviously superior to that of individuals. During the earliest scrambles for supremacy between Eastern and Western civilizations, the Roman-Nordic alliance could not defeat the brave Huns who, after all, fled to Western Europe after being beaten by the troops of King Wu of the Han dynasty.

Great Achievements in Ancient and Modern Chinese Monetary History

1. The world's first cast coins originated in China during the Shang dynasty.

2. The earliest monetary chronology in the world came from China's Southern Song dynasty.
3. China was the first country in the world to use paper money.
4. The *jiaozi* of the Northern Song dynasty was the earliest official paper money in the world.
5. The Zhongtong-reign currency of the Yuan dynasty is by far the earliest paper money in existence today.
6. The paper money of the Great Ming is the largest banknote in the world.
7. The monetary law of the Yuan dynasty featured the earliest self-contained circulation system for paper money in the world.
8. The essay "Persuasions on Coining Money" on monetary issues by Jia Yi of the Western Han dynasty is the earliest writing on this topic in the world.

As befitted this demarcation between civilizations, the Western currency was a standard system that came along a natural course of evolution and was based on popular trust in it. By contrast, the paper currencies jiaozi, feiqian, and the negotiable paper for salt transactions that evolved during the Song dynasty were forms of credit guaranteed not by precious metals but by the belief that the collective could ensure the safety of a holder's properties.

The future undoubtedly holds a variety of scenarios for economic development. With Eastern and Western civilizations intermingling and interacting along an uncharted road, and with the development of the Chinese economy and the dissemination of Chinese culture, the Renminbi will continue to reach out to the world step by step.

It can be expected that within the framework in which diverse civilizations coexist, Renminbi is bound to become a major economic symbol of the "China element" in the global economy.

CHAPTER 2

THE CORNERSTONE OF CHINESE CURRENCY: GROWTH WITHOUT CRISIS

The structure of the international monetary system is consistent with the economic strength of major developed countries. International currencies have always been the currencies of rich countries. Thirty years of economic growth without crisis has not only caught world attention but also become the economic cornerstone for the Chinese yuan.

Growth without crisis does not mean that an economy grows without any problems. It means that any problem will not further evolve into a major economic downturn, and the economy will still maintain high long-term growth in spite of ups and downs. Since the outbreak of the first economic crisis in England in 1825, the world has witnessed 21 major economic or financial crises that swept almost all countries in the world. However, as one of the developing countries, China maintained continuous high growth during the reform and opening up over the last 30 years without a typical economic or financial crisis.

In recent years, China's high-speed yet stable economic growth drew close attention from many economists. Nobel Prize laureate for economics Milton Friedman once claimed that anyone who was able to explain China's economic phenomenon could win the Nobel Prize in Economics. After the latest outbreak of the global financial crisis, the model of growth without crisis has drawn even more attention.

Sustained Economic Growth

Since the start of the Chinese reform and opening up, China has achieved economic development that caught the attention of the world. The average growth rate of Chinese GDP over the past 30 years is approximately 10 percent (see Figure 2.1). Based on historical data, China witnessed the highest economic growth rate during this period of time, enjoying the longest growth benefiting the largest number of people in the history of human beings (see Table 2.1). Its growth rate is more than five times that of the global GDP per capita growth rate of 1.5 percent for the same time (see Figure 2.1). According to estimates from the World Bank, it took Great Britain 58 years (from 1780 to 1838), the United States 47 years (from 1839 to 1886), Japan 34 years (from 1885 to 1919), and South Korea 11 years (from 1966 to 1977) to double income per capita. But it took China only 8.6 years to do that.

By 2009 China's nominal GDP reached US$4.19 trillion, which was exceeded only by the United States and Japan. China's nominal GDP accounted for 8 percent of the global economic aggregate. As a matter of fact, the strong Chinese economic growth is not just about historical data. In order to objectively evaluate China's achievement in raising income per capita and improving its society, the best way is to make a field trip to China in person. The World Bank report *China 2020: Development Challenges in the New Century* mentioned "that

Table 2.1 Chinese GDP Growth Rate and GDP Per Capita, 1978-2009

Time	Countries
1870s	Germany, Belgium, Netherlands, Austria
1880s	Germany, Finland, Austria, Denmark
1970s	Botswana, Malta, Singapore, South Korea
1980s	South Korea, China, Botswana, Thailand
1990s	China (10.3%), Vietnam (7.9%), Singapore (7.8%), Ireland (7.8%)

Sources: The nineteenth-century data is from Mancur Olson, "Why Some Countries Are Rich and Others Poor," *Comparison* 7 (2003): 21–38. The 1990 data is the average GDP growth rate, from the World Bank, World Development Report 2002, pp. 236–237.

Figure 2.1. Chinese GDP Growth Rate and GDP Per Capita, 1978–2009

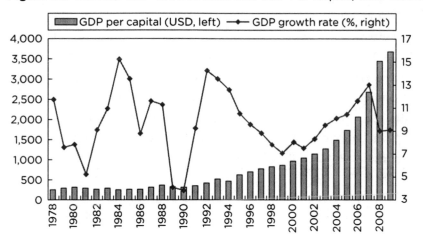

it only takes China one generation to achieve what other countries did over centuries. For a country with a population exceeding the total of Africa's and Latin America's, that is the most impressive development in this century."

Stages of Chinese Economic Development After the Reform and Opening Up

Overall, China's economic development has gone through roughly three stages since the reform and opening up:

- The first stage, from 1978 to 1991, was characterized by tremendous political swings. Economic development during this period was relatively cyclical, corresponding to political events, such as a new administration or a political party convention.
- The second stage, from 1992 to 1999, was a period with rapid expansion. In 1992, the central party committee targeted a socialist market economy as the objective for China's economic restructuring. With the development of non-state-owned sectors, constant inflows of foreign investment, and continuous increase in exports, China entered a period of high-speed economic

growth. The average economic growth rate in this period was 10.9 percent.

- The third stage, from 2000 to now, is a period of stable and high-speed growth. After 2000, the Chinese socialist market economy was basically established, and the economic growth pattern and industrial structure were changing in a more optimal way. With the proposal of innovative national strategies, China entered a new economic development period characterized by low carbon, economy of scale, stability, and innovations.

With the acceleration of economic and financial globalization, China as an open economy plays a more and more important role in the international political and economic arena. When the global crisis wreaked havoc on major economies, China's economy performed rather well. China's GDP growth rate reached 9.1 percent in 2009, and its contributions to global economic recovery exceeded 50 percent. As this large oriental country with a long history is gradually becoming a global economic growth engine, the sign Made in China all over the world is an important signal declaring that China has become an integral part of the global economy.

Chinese GDP in 2010 ranked second in the world, but that does not mean Chinese economic power is top ranked too. Chinese GDP is only one-third that of the United States, the largest economy. According to the latest data from the International Monetary Fund (IMF), Chinese GDP per capita was only $3,566, ranked ninety-ninth in the world. Using $8,000 as the world average GDP per capita, Chinese GDP per capita was only 45 percent of the world average. Therefore, relatively low GDP per capita indicates that China is still a typical developing country despite increasing economic output and power in recent years, and it still must close a relatively large gap to catch up with developed countries.

Growing Foreign Trade

"If we could persuade each Chinese to stretch his shirt for an inch, factories in Lancashire would have a large enough market for their products," a British writer wrote back in 1840. As a large, open economy with 1.3 billion people, high-quality and inexpensive labor, and a huge, constantly developing domestic market, China is attracting foreign companies. Foreign firms come to China to build manufacturing facilities and research centers, trying to grab China's market share as well as the world market to take advantage of low cost and economies of scale.

With high-speed economic growth and in-depth integration into the global economy, China's foreign trade has jumped. Since its official entry into the World Trade Organization (WTO) in 2002, China has maintained an annual increase in foreign trade of more than 20 percent. China's imports and exports have quadrupled (see Figure 2.2.) Made-in-China products are sold all over the world, and China has been gradually confirmed as an important trading nation. For the time being, China is the largest exporting country and the second-largest importing country, with its total trade volume reaching US$2.21 trillion.

Increasing exports and imports not only contributed to Chinese economic growth but also stimulated global economic growth. It acted as the main engine for the economic growth of other Asian regions and neighboring countries. China purchased large quantities of equipment and technologies from Japan, South Korea, Germany,

Figure 2.2 China's Import and Export Trade

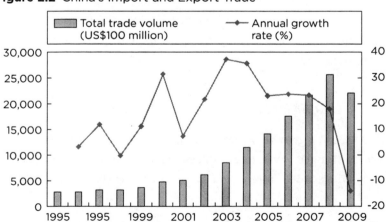

and the United States while building its modern economic infrastructures. Morgan Stanley's chief economist Stephen Roach thought that because of rapid Chinese economic growth, neighboring economies had formed an Asian economic model centered on mainland China. Most of these countries wanted to benefit from skyrocketing trade volumes with China.

According to the report titled *Studies on China's Foreign Trade Development Strategy in the Post-crisis Era*, lately issued by the National Institute of the Ministry of Commerce, China will strive to double commodity and service trade in the coming decade. By 2020, China's total trade volume will have reached approximately US$5.3 trillion, of which commodity trade will be US$4.3 trillion and service trade will be US$1 trillion. The report pointed out that China's foreign trade would become strong instead of large in the coming 20 years, and China would achieve the goal of becoming a strong trading power by 2030.

The increase of trade volumes was accompanied by China's active and balanced multilateral trade. On January 1, 2010, the China–ASEAN Free Trade Area (CAFTA) was established, which created a market with 1.9 billion in population, US$6 trillion in GDP, and over US$4.5 trillion in total trade volume.

Thanks to low trade costs, industrial optimization, and the integration of regional economies, CAFTA will maintain an average growth rate of 25 percent in the next decade. With CAFTA as its center, China's multilateral trade will expand to Mongolia and Russia. Meanwhile, China's trade with the United States, the European Union (EU), Japan, South Korea, and other nations will continue to develop in a more balanced and stable way.

The Chinese Model That Draws World Attention

Over 30 years of growth without crisis has greatly increased China's economic strength. The great success of the Chinese economy has attracted more and more developing countries to learn from the

Chinese model; how to successfully adopt the Chinese model has become a popular issue among economists. China learned from its own conditions and carried out economic transformation step by step, achieving great success in the end. Reality tells us that step-by-step reform is a key factor that enabled China to achieve growth without crisis in the past 30 years.

The Chinese model of economic success and economic development has been summarized as the Beijing Consensus. The transformation from the Washington Consensus to the Beijing Consensus shows that the success of the Chinese model is not only an economic phenomenon but also a change of the developmental concept, which claims that every nation has the right and ability to find the most suitable way for its development.

The Washington Consensus and the Beijing Consensus

The Washington Consensus is a series of political and economic theories proposed in 1989 for transforming economies such as those of Latin American and Eastern European countries. The consensus covers the following 10 aspects:

1. Strengthen fiscal discipline, cut deficits, reduce inflation, and maintain macroeconomic stability.
2. Direct government spending to economically efficient fields and areas that can help improve income distributions, such as culture, education, public health, and infrastructure.
3. Execute taxation reform, lower marginal tax rates, and broaden the taxation basis.
4. Promote the market-oriented interest rate system.
5. Adopt a competitive exchange rate system.
6. Promote free trade and the open market.
7. Loosen controls over foreign investment.
8. Privatize state-owned enterprises.

9. Relax government controls.
10. Protect private property rights.

Noam Chomsky, a famous American scholar, pointed out in his book *Neoliberalism and Global Order* that the neoliberal Washington Consensus refers to a series of market-oriented theories. The theories were formulated and implemented in various ways by the U.S. government and international organizations controlled by the United States.

As the Washington Consensus was failing, the opposite Beijing Consensus emerged as a macroeconomic theory. Joshua Cooper Ramo, senior editor of Time magazine and senior consultant of Goldman Sachs, a U.S. investment bank, published a research paper with London's Foreign Policy Centre and pointed out that China, through innovations and bold actions, had achieved a development pattern that was suitable for its national conditions. He named this pattern the Beijing Consensus. Ramo claimed that the Beijing Consensus was characterized by hard work; active innovation; bold actions such as establishing special economic zones, firmly upholding sovereignty and national interests (as in handling the Taiwan issue); step-by-step development such as trial and error and advancing cautiously or "crossing the river by touching stones" in Chinese); and building up energy and possessing the instruments of unusual power, such as accumulating huge foreign exchange reserves.

History tells us that the economy is connected to culture, and economic development will definitely lead to cultural prosperity. As Chinese international standing and influence continue to grow, learning Chinese language and culture has enjoyed great popularity in many countries. At present, the number of people who are learning Chinese is growing at a rate of 50 percent, and in some countries the rate has even doubled. By 2010, the number of people who speak Chinese as their first foreign language will reach 50 million. If the growth rate continues, it is estimated that the number will reach 200,000 million in 2020. Chinese will surpass French to be the second most popular language in the world after English.

The Economic Foundation for Growth Without Crisis

Generally speaking, in the coming decades China will have strong liquidity internationally, a solid banking system, an effective financial firewall, a high and stable savings rate, and a huge market with differential capacities. These five factors will build a solid economic foundation for future growth in China without financial crises.

The first factor is strong international liquidity. In a modern economy, a nation's foreign exchange reserves affect not only its payment capacity in international trade but also the ability to maintain financial stability at special times such as a financial crisis. By the end of 2009, China's foreign exchange reserve has reached US$2.3991 trillion and has ranked number one in the world (see Figure 2.3).

The second factor is a solid banking system. Banks take a leading role in the Chinese financial system. In recent years, after financial reforms, Chinese banks have significantly improved their risk management and sustainable growth abilities. According to statistics from the China Banking Regulatory Commission, at the end of June 2009 total assets held by Chinese banks exceeded ¥70 trillion,

Figure 2.3 China's Foreign Exchange Reserve

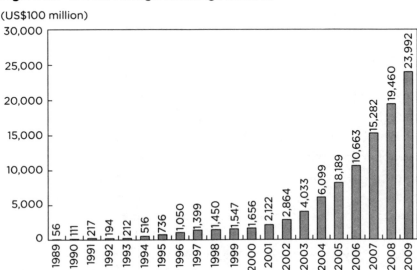

(US$100 million)

which was 388 times those in 1978. There were a total of 219 well-capitalized banks, and their assets accounted for 99.9 percent of total assets held by all commercial banks. Their nonperforming loan ratio was 1.7 percent and commercial banks' provisioning coverage ratio was 134.3 percent. Risk management capabilities have improved significantly. According to data published by the British magazine *Banker*, 84 Chinese banks ranked among the top 1,000 banks in the world in 2010 (see Table 2.2 for 25 of them). The total capital of these 84 Chinese banks accounted for 9 percent of the capital of the 1,000 top banks, and pretax interest income accounted for 25 percent. The Industrial and Commercial Bank of China (ICBC), which ranks seventh in terms of total capital, is the most profitable bank in the world. Therefore, in terms of capital, nonperforming loan ratio, and profitability, a robust Chinese banking system has been formed.

The third factor is the effective financial firewall. The Chinese financial system has not been completely open to the world, and the Chinese yuan is freely convertible only for current account transactions. Although the regulation of the capital account has been somewhat loosened, China is still relatively high in regulations and controls among countries in the world, which means the financial firewall still plays an important role. In the next step of reform, China will gradually open up its financial system, improve financial system designs, strengthen prudent macroeconomic supervision, and enhance risk management and control initiatives.

The fourth factor is the high and stable savings rate. Savings are the main source of capital. In general, a high savings rate means a high investment rate, which on one hand directly increases demand and on the other hand promotes supply-side economic growth. Based on the Harrod-Domar model, the savings rate is in direct proportion to the economic growth rate. The higher the savings rate, the faster an economy grows. Since the 1990s, China has enjoyed high savings rates (see Figure 2.4). Large savings are a strong impetus in support of economic growth and strengthen risk management capability.

The last factor is a large market with differential capacities. Despite 30 years of high economic growth, China's economic growth

Table 2.2 Global Rankings of Chinese Commercial Banks (millions of U.S. dollars)

Ranking	Chinese Name	English Name	Tier One Capital	Total Assets
7	中国工商银行	Industrial and Commercial Bank of China	91,111	1,725,938
14	中国银行	Bank of China	73,667	1,281,183
15	中国建设银行	China Construction Bank	71,974	1,409,355
28	中国农业银行	Agricultural Bank of China	39,786	1,026,021
49	交通银行	Bank of Communications	22,625	484,628
67	中信银行	China CITIC Bank	14,526	259,956
80	中国民生银行	China Minsheng Banking Corp., Ltd.	12,998	208,897
81	招商银行	China Merchants Bank	12,928	302,853
97	中国兴业银行	Industrial Bank	11,279	195,097
108	上海浦东发展银行	Shanghai Pudong Development Bank	9,546	237,649
136	中国光大银行	China Everbright Bank	6,799	175,397
155	北京银行	Bank of Beijing	5,372	78,127
178	华夏银行	Hua Xia Bank	4,328	123,818
218	广东发展银行	Guangdong Development Bank	3,147	97,608
226	上海银行	Bank of Shanghai	3,000	68,252
231	深圳发展银行	Shenzhen Development Bank	2,955	86,086
292	江苏银行	Bank of Jiangsu	2,196	48,425
299	平安银行	Ping An Bank	2,096	32,319
339	上海农村商业银行	Shanghai Rural Commercial Bank	1,810	31,035
349	南京银行	Bank of Nanjing	1,754	21,838
356	徽商银行	Huishang Bank	1,719	23,784

(continued)

35

Table 2.2 Global Rankings of Chinese Commercial Banks (millions of U.S. dollars) (continued)

Ranking	Chinese Name	English Name	Tier One Capital	Total Assets
377	广州农村商业银行	Guangzhou Rural Commercial Bank	1,574	27,195
391	恒丰银行	Evergrowing Bank	1,483	31,306
395	杭州银行	Bank of Hangzhou	1,465	21,966
419	宁波银行	Bank of Ningbo	1,362	23,923

Source: British magazine *Banker.*

is still unbalanced between urban and rural areas. Due to disparities between urban and rural economic structures and economic development imbalances between different regions, a huge market with differential capacities will gradually demonstrate its advantages during China's transformation in the next decades from economic growth driven by investments to growth driven by domestic demand. The transformation process will not only help transform the economic growth model and form a more stable and balanced economic structure but also enhance the capacity to tap into economic potential and resist internal and external financial impacts.

Figure 2.4 China's National Savings Rate

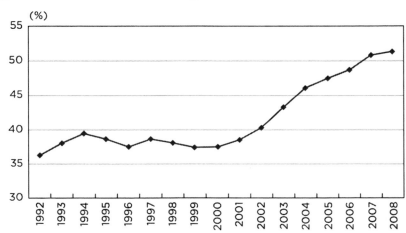

As a matter of fact, Chinese economic growth has the foundation to exist without crisis and maintain a sustainable high speed. First, Chinese GDP per capita is still very low at present. Based on economic growth experience from other countries, a small quantitative base leads to a large growth rate whereas a large quantitative base leads to a small growth rate. What's more, China is currently in the industrialization stage. According to international experience, the growth rate of this period can be relatively high. It can be forecasted that due to the small quantitative base, China will maintain the trend of high economic growth for quite a long time in the future.

Economic Growth During Industrialization: International Practice and China's National Condition

Economists have done specific studies on the criteria by which to classify industrialization stages. According to Hollis Chenery's research, industrialization is a stage at which per-capita GDP ranges from US$200 to US$3,600. The primary stage of industrialization is believed to see GDP per capita ranging from US$200 to US$400; the intermediate stage, from US$400 to US$1,500; and the advanced stage, from US$1,500 to US$3,600. At the beginning of the 1980s, China's GDP per capita reached US$200, and GDP per capita kept growing year over year. In 2009, GDP per capita was US$3,678. According to Chenery's standard, China was in the process of industrialization during the last 20 years.

Based on the development of other countries in the world, countries in the industrialization process enjoyed relatively high economic growth rates. For example, based on the World Bank's statistics for all nations in 1997, industrialized countries whose per-capita GDP was between US$200 and US$5,000 had an average GDP growth rate of 4.9 percent. For countries with per-capita GPD of US$5,000 to US$10,000, the rate was 4.2 percent. For countries with per-capita GDP over US$10,000, the rate was 3.7 percent. It can be seen that the economic growth rates at various industrialized stages are different.

Of course, industrialization is a favorable condition during a nation's economic growth, but it alone is not sufficient. There are many countries with GDP per capita between US$200 and US$5,000. Although these countries normally have higher economic growth rates than other countries, the economic growth rates of the countries within this income per capita range differ among themselves.

Second, urban construction, the transportation system, and the increase of population, as well as household consumption during urbanization, are factors that can promote economic growth. After the reform and opening up, China has seen rapid urbanization. Although Chinese urbanization is below the global average, it is catching up quickly (see Figure 2.5). Under normal circumstances, the Chinese urban population will reach approximately 0.9 billion by 2020. Total consumption will reach RMB23.5 trillion in 2020 (prices not adjusted for inflation), and purchases for investment purposes will reach RMB14.4 trillion. Urbanization will provide favorable market conditions for large-scale industrial investment. In spite of world market volatility, China will have sufficient domestic demand to stimulate its own economic growth.

Figure 2.5 The Urbanization Rate of China and the World

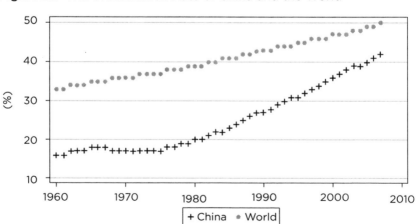

Urbanization is closely associated with economic development and economic structure. The actuality of other countries in the world shows that urbanization is conducive to improving the economic structure, increasing domestic demand, and developing tertiary industry. Studies conducted on urbanization and economic levels have proved that there is a dynamic and stable relationship among urbanization, income per capita, and capital per capita. Based on the relationship, the Chinese urbanization level will exceed 60 percent in the coming 10 years.

Huge Market Demand from Urbanization: The International Experience

Almost all modern nations have to go through high-speed urbanization, which is integrally related to the economy and economic structure. Sound urbanization should be interactively related to economic growth. There is significant correlation between urbanization and economic growth, which can be illustrated with the S-curve in Figure 2.6. According to the curve, China is in the fastest urbanization stage for the time being.

Figure 2.6 The S-curve of Urbanization

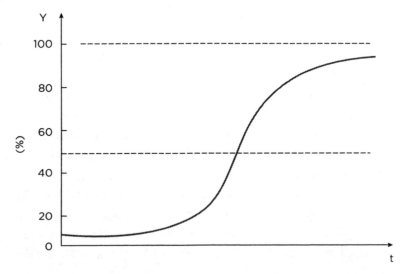

According to the economic growth situations in some East Asian countries and regions, restructuring takes place when the urbanization level is 35 to 55 percent and GDP per capita is between US$1,000 and US$3,000. It is still a period of fast economic growth. For example, the growth rate of South Korea averaged 3.84 percent from 1953 to 1962, 8.48 percent from 1962 to 1991, and 5.76 percent from 1991 to 2000. South Korea has had rapid growth for 38 years. Singapore's average growth rate was 5.74 percent from 1960 to 1965, 9.86 percent from 1965 to 1984, and 7.18 percent from 1984 to 2000. Singapore has had fast growth for 35 years. The growth rate of Taiwan averaged 7.92 percent during the period 1951 to 1962, 9.48 percent for the period 1962 to 1987, and 6.59 percent for the period 1987 to 2000. The Taiwan region has seen rapid growth for 49 years. The features of future economic restructuring and changes of GDP per capita in mainland China demonstrate that China is right in the middle of a stage with fast economic growth.

Actually, these five elements mentioned above determine that the Chinese economic and financial system can demonstrate great elasticity and self-repair capability during a crisis. To some extent, these elements also lay an economic foundation for Chinese economic growth without crisis in the coming decades. Japan maintained rapid economic growth for 40 years from after World War II till the end of the 1980s. Four Asian Tigers also maintained rapid growth for 40 years from the end of the 1950s until the recent financial crisis. Economists who are familiar with China's national conditions predict that Chinese high-speed economic growth can last another 20 years.

Based on China's current economic growth cycles, the macroeconomic forum of Renmin University of China conducted a scenario analysis of Chinese economic fluctuations during the period 2009–2010 and economic growth trend for the period 2013–2032. According to the analysis, predicted annual Chinese real GDP growth rates for 2009–2012 and predicted Chinese annual average real GDP growth rates for 2013–2022 and 2023–2032 are shown in Table 2.3.

Table 2.3 China's Real GDP Growth Rate: 2009–2012 and 2013–2032 (percent)

Economic Cycle	2008	2009	2010	2011	2012	2008–2012 Average
Mild resurgence/ steady expansion (S)	9.00	9.04	9.85	10.09	10.43	9.68
Slow resurgence/ aggressive expansion (J)	9.00	7.74	9.61	10.34	11.02	9.54
Swift resurgence/ quick drop (U)	9.00	9.68	10.90	9.53	9.06	9.63
	2013–2022			2023–2032		
Max	8.82			7.65		
Trend (T)	8.54			7.48		
Min	8.26			7.32		

Source: Data from Luo Laijun (2009).
Note: Mild recovery and steady expansion cycle (S model) for 2009–2010 and historical annual average economic growth rate trend (T) for 2013–2032 constitute the basis for the prediction of Chinese economic growth rate in 2009–2032. Based on economic cycles (S model) in the leading period and the historical annual average economic growth trend (T), the annual average economic growth trend (T) as well as max and min values are predicted by rolling over data one period after another.

The predictions show that the trend of China's GDP growth rate will be as high as 7 to 8 percent in the next two decades.

Developing the Nation's Long-Term Strategy of Growth Without Crisis: Finance and Industrial Economy

The analysis of developing a long-term national strategy of growth without crisis for China during the postcrisis period can be undertaken from two aspects, finance and industrial economy.

Finance

From the finance perspective, China should consider growth without crisis as the core of its overall financial strategy, whether trying to deal with the global financial crisis or to prevent a crisis from happening in the future.

First, among the underlying causes of and reactions to the global financial crisis, imbalanced trade, ineffective supervision, and inappropriate monetary policies, which have been mentioned repeatedly, are main culprits. The real cause of a modern financial crisis, however, is the economic cycles that are deeply rooted in the global economic and financial system, as shown by financial crises during the last 20 years. With this understanding, China must conduct the reform of the financial monitoring and regulatory system from the following aspects.

1. *Monitoring and regulatory objectives:* Priority must be placed on macroeconomic stability while upholding the opening-up policy. Efficiency must be subordinated to stability in the financial system.

2. *Organizational structures:* China should have a monitoring and regulatory system that is closely connected to the central bank to promote the balance between stability and efficiency of internal factors within the financial system, while using effective economic regulation and controls to achieve coordination between the financial system and the industrial economy.

3. *Monitoring and regulatory methods:* China should reform current methods that are based on rules by researching and formulating countercyclical regulatory methods. Potential methods include more flexible requirements on capital and establishment of countercyclical loss reserves.

4. *Coordination between different policies:* Financial monitoring and regulatory policies should be consistent with monetary policies. China should monitor the major macroeconomic and financial index by establishing an accurate, effective, and timely monitoring system and an early-warning mechanism to detect various normal unstable factors as early as possible, such as sharply rising asset prices, high financial leverage, and unusual offshore borrowings and capital flows.

Second, from the perspective of developing a national financial strategy during the aftermath of the financial crisis, the world is facing changing global economic power, and the global financial system, which has been centered on the United States and the U.S. dollar since World War II, is facing restructuring. During this process, the strategy to develop the Chinese financial system must consider Chinese national conditions and the current stage of development, and must organically connect internal industrial needs, external regulations and controls, and industrial sectors to achieve their interactive support.

1. In the process of opening and developing the financial industry, China must maintain appropriate controls to ensure the stability of the financial system and avoid financial issues arising from global financial liberalization, economic transformation, and opening up to the outside world.

2. The development of the financial industry should be undertaken steadily, step by step, with varying levels and different emphasis. While further reforming the banking industry, China must further develop the capital market, utilize its resource allocation function, and promote balanced development of the banking industry and the capital market.

3. In building a modern financial system, China must fully consider national conditions and focus on fundamental regulations, including information disclosure, corporate governance, transparency requirements, deposit insurance, risk management, and bankruptcy mechanisms. China must allow the efficiency mechanism to play its role more smoothly, strengthen the multilayer risk control and automatic stabilization system, and ultimately achieve long-term dynamic balance between efficiency and stability.

Third, the global financial crisis demonstrates that financial freedom contributes to long-term economic growth and financial stability but will likely cause financial crises in the short run if a nation ignores its abilities and jumps ahead of its stage of development. Therefore, the method and depth of financial freedom are critical. For most developing countries, a decline in financial controls by the state is the main reason why a financial crisis cannot be controlled or avoided in time. From the perspective of the longer historical period, developing countries were more susceptible to financial crises. The reasons can also be traced back to the fact that most developing countries failed to manage the degree of financial freedom, that is, the depth and pace of financial freedom, which eventually led to sharply declining macroeconomic control power and crisis control power.

Therefore, a developing country must focus on the long term to construct a more useful system to detect the crisis at an early stage and adopt preemptive measures. Such a system must include financial freedom, financial stability, and state regulation and control, and it must allow these three aspects to interact. After the recent global financial crisis, China must appropriately adjust the pace of financial freedom to strengthen the ability of the state to control the risks in the financial system and take proactive actions while continuing economic reforms and opening up to the world.

Industrial Economy

If growth without crisis can be regarded as the core of the financial strategy, China must regard economic restructuring and transformation of its economic development model as the core of its growth strategy from the perspective of industrial economy, whenever China tries to mitigate impacts from the current financial crisis in the short run or to lay a firm foundation for stable economic development in the long run. Focusing on this issue, China can concentrate on the breakthrough of the following aspects to achieve economic development in the future.

The first aspect is associated with industrial restructuring. In the preliminary stage of industrialization, due to high demand for production and investment, the market is fraught with many enterprises that are characterized by high input cost, high energy consumption, high pollution, and low efficiency (or Three Highs and One Low enterprises). These enterprises have contributed to economic and employment growth but also caused environmental and ecological damages detrimental to the sustainable development of the economy. The strategy for industrial development in the next stage calls for China to gradually increase industrial structural levels; abandon the old way of primarily relying on obsolete imported technologies and the gradual transformation of recipient industries; adopt a new way of industrialization with high technology, high efficiency, high added value, and energy efficiency; create a virtuous cycle from industry to investment and further to talents and finally to efficiency; transform low-end production factors to high-end ones; and achieve the accumulation of high-level production elements. In accordance with these thoughts, China must support new industries during the next stage of industrialization, not labor-intensive industries characterized by Three Highs and One Low. China must promote capital-intensive and technology-intensive enterprises, as well as some labor-intensive enterprises suitable for China's unique situations, to reach the goal of accelerating industrial transformations and taking advantage of comparative advantages while alleviating unemployment pressures.

The second aspect is associated with the adjustment of regional structures. The imbalance of regional economic development is an issue that requires prompt solution during economic development and transformation. Development has differed between the eastern and the western regions for a long time, with the western region consistently lagging behind. Development also differs between urban and rural areas, with rural areas significantly lagging behind urban areas. Unlike regional imbalance, the imbalance between urban and rural areas has continued to grow since the 1990s, especially in the western region. As China ushers in a new stage of economic development, it is important to implement the strategy of "developing the west" and stimulating domestic demand by utilizing the advantage of belated development in the western region to generate Chinese economic growth for the next few generations. The west enjoys the advantages of large population, vast land, abundant natural resources, and great potential for future economic growth. China must take advantage of natural resources in the western region and guide regional development with appropriate policies, regulations, and planning to establish a new resource-based economic model and hence develop a new resource-based economic ring, which will help to alleviate regional imbalance, urban and rural imbalance, and personal income imbalance and to build a solid foundation for long-term Chinese economic growth.

At a crucial stage of building a moderately prosperous society, China proposed the major strategy of becoming an innovation-oriented country by 2020, based on unique national situations and economic developmental needs. This means that science and technology will become the foundation for future economic and societal development.[1] In terms of the stages of economic development, China has entered the final industrialization stage. In order to achieve higher innovation-oriented economic growth, China must break away from the resource-based economic growth model and adopt one that is based on science and technology. Building an innovation-oriented country requires increasing contributions from science and technology, including three important steps: (1) vigorously improve knowledge and encourage innovative thinking, (2) transform knowledge into patents in order to connect knowledge with production, and (3) reach a consensus on economic growth and transform technological advancement and patents into economic growth. Currently China's economic growth faces the issue of relatively low efficiency. There is still a long way to go to build an innovation-oriented country and achieve the transformation of economic growth by 2020. The first 20 years of this century are a period of important strategic opportunity for Chinese economic and societal development as well as the development of science and technology. Only by raising independent innovation ability and changing the investment-dependent and resource-dependent growth model to one driven by innovation can China fundamentally stimulate economic vitality and achieve sustainable and stable long-term economic growth.

CHAPTER 3

CHINESE MONETARY POLICY

To stabilize currency value and thereby to promote economic growth is the statutory objective of the Chinese monetary policy.

The implementation of correct and rational monetary policy enables China to successfully achieve crisis-proof economic growth and the stability of the Chinese economy.

Moving from state-mandated plans to indirect regulations, China has clearly demonstrated that its monetary policy is oriented toward the market.

Monetary policy refers to a central bank's various policies and measures that influence the macroeconomy through money supplies in order to achieve the objective of macroeconomic regulation. Monetary policy is an important part of a nation's macroeconomic policy and it is also one of the important instruments to achieve macroeconomic regulation and goals. Monetary policy aims to stabilize prices, develop the economy, and achieve full employment and an international balance of payments through a series of monetary policy instruments. Monetary policy is usually composed of many parts, such as its goals, instruments, execution mechanisms, and effects.

China's Central Bank: The People's Bank of China

On December 1, 1948, the North China Bank, Beihai Bank, and Northwestern Peasants' Bank merged to form the People's Bank of China and began to issue Renminbi. However, the People's Bank of China did not serve as a central bank in the beginning. In 1969 the People's Bank of China merged into the Ministry of Finance and had no real power. In 1978 the People's Bank of China was separated from the Ministry of Finance. The economic reforms that started in 1978 set China onto the road toward a market economy. In September 1983 the State Council decided to approve the People's Bank of China to perform the exclusive role of a central bank, which led to the final establishment of the Chinese central bank system. On March 18, 1995, the third session of the Eighth National People's Congress passed the Law of the People's Republic of China on the People's Bank of China. From that time on, the People's Bank of China was legally designated as the central bank of China.

Before 1978 China practiced central planning of the economic system, under which macroeconomic regulations and controls were realized by planning and mandatory financial means while monetary and credit means were secondary. In such a centralized financial model, the People's Bank of China performed all the functions of a central bank, a specialized bank, an ordinary bank, and a nonbanking financial institution. The monetary policy was actually a comprehensive credit policy. In the 1980s, as the traditional planned economic system was transformed into a market economic system, the operations of financial reform and monetary policies changed. In 1984, after the People's Bank of China assumed the role of a central bank, the central bank system officially came into being in China and a new monetary policy began to take shape. During this period, the central planning management system was gradually changed to macroeconomic regulations and controls characterized by direct regulation and control by the state. Although planned management of credit and cash remained in a leading role, indirect financial instruments began to have some influences.

With the development of the Chinese financial system reform since the 1990s, monetary policy gradually shifted toward indirect regulations and controls. The Chinese monetary policy operations from 1993 to 2010 can be broken into four periods (see Table 3.1). From

Table 3.1 The Evolution of Chinese Monetary Policy, 1979–2010

Stage	Characteristics	Main Content and Operations
1979–1983	Monetary policy of the planned management system	In this period, monetary policy was still managed under the central planning system. Since the country was a highly centralized and planned economy, the amount of currency in circulation, prices, and economic growth were controlled by the government. Monetary policy's effect could not be seen. But the economic index showed that monetary policy was centered on stabilizing the currency's value while giving consideration to economic growth.
1984–1992	Monetary policy in the macroeconomic management system	After 1984 the People's Bank of China began to perform the role of a central bank, and the central-planning economic system was changed to a macroeconomic regulation system based on regulations and controls by the state. In 1988 serious inflation took place. In the second half of 1989, the central bank adopted extremely tight monetary policies.
1993–1997	Monetary policy aiming at anti-inflation	At the beginning of the 1990s, China began to see evidence of economic bubbles. Money supplies exceeded normal amounts and the inflation rate hit double digits. To fight severe inflation in 1993 and 1994, China implemented macroeconomic policies to realize an economic soft landing. The primary monetary policies during this period included bringing order to the financial market, adjusting monetary policy objectives, implementing new monetary instruments, flexibly utilizing interest rates as leverage, and unifying foreign exchange rates. The Chinese economy successfully achieved a soft landing after four years of macroeconomic controls.

(continued)

1993 to 1997, an economic soft landing was successfully achieved by implementing a moderately tight monetary policy to fight inflation. From 1998 to 2002, monetary policy was moderately loose, with an aim to control deflation in order to promote economic growth. From

Table 3.1 The Evolution of Chinese Monetary Policy, 1979–2010 (continued)

Stage	Characteristics	Main Content and Operations
1998–2002	Monetary policy aiming at anti-inflation	In January 1998 the central bank terminated controls on credit sizes, and the influence of monetary policy improved unprecedentedly. In 1998, when China witnessed deflation, the purpose of China's monetary policy was evidently aimed at promoting economic growth. From 1998 to 2002, the People's Bank of China lowered interest rates substantially, expanded the range of loan interest rates, enhanced open market operations, terminated control over loan quotas, and flexibly applied credit policies and credit restructuring to generate economic growth.
2003–2008	Monetary policy aiming at anti-inflation and economic overheating	At the beginning of 2003, to fight against the excessive increase of credit available in the economy, and irrational investment and low-quality expansion in some industries and regions, the People's Bank of China maintained monetary policy stability and continuity while implementing stable monetary policies. The specific measures were to steadily promote market economy, enhance the capacity to regulate the monetary base through open market operations, raise reserve requirement ratios and implement the system of differential deposit reserve ratios, strengthen real estate credit management, and provide appropriate guidance to financial institutions at the right time.

2003 to 2008, the main monetary policy objective was to fight inflation and to control the overheated economy. From 2009 until the present, monetary policy is moderately loose to meet the demand of economic stability and recovery after the global financial crisis.

In summary, in the processes of formulating and implementing monetary policies since the 1990s, China has gradually decreased direct regulations and controls while continuously increasing indirect regulations and controls. The ultimate goal of the monetary policy has

Table 3.1 The Evolution of Chinese Monetary Policy, 1979–2010 (continued)

Stage	Characteristics	Main Content and Operations
2009 until now	Expansionary monetary policy aiming at maintaining growth	As the global financial crisis was getting worse and the Chinese economy suffered, on November 11, 2008, the Chinese government made a major adjustment to the macroeconomic regulation and control policy, determining to implement a proactive fiscal policy and moderate expansionary monetary policy by launching 4 trillion yuan to stimulate domestic demand in the following two years in order to promote economic growth. In 2009, China's monetary policy was the most accommodative in the last 10 years. The amount of the M2 money supply increased 27.7%, which was 20 basis points higher than the sum of the GDP growth rate and consumer price index growth rate. Newly increased Renminbi loans were close to 10 trillion yuan, which almost doubled the size of the prior year.

been to stabilize the currency value and thereby to promote economic growth. Monetary policy's intermediate and operational targets have turned from credit sizes to money supply and monetary base. Indirect regulation and control instruments, such as deposit reserve ratios, interest rates, central bank loans, discounting, and open market operations, have gradually increased. Currently, China has already established the indirect regulation and control system through regulating the monetary base by using various monetary policy instruments to reach the intermediate goal of controlling the money supply and the ultimate goal of stabilizing the currency value.

The Chinese Credit Plan and Its Transformation

In the planned economy, China nationalized the manufacturing and service industries, achieved agricultural collectivization, and executed the central planning of material production by manufacturing units as well as the central allocation of materials. Capital expenditures were funded by the Ministry of Finance and corporate profits were submitted to the state.

The function of currency was limited; it was confined to payroll payments, procurement of agricultural products, and retail transactions. The commodity price, interest rate, and exchange rate were strictly controlled by the state. Accordingly, China did not have a clear intermediate target for monetary policy. Credit and cash plans had been important policy instruments for the Chinese central bank.

The credit plan was an important tool for the central bank to control the money supply. In the past, the credit plan system was complicated and could be classified into five levels, namely, retail credit plans, the central bank's annual lending plans, the national bank's credit plans, credit plans by other financial institutions, and direct financing plans by various enterprises. Retail credit plans that were directly involved with the credit activities of the whole society were formulated by the headquarters of the People's Bank of China, submitted to the State Council, and distributed after approval. The headquarters of the People's Bank of China was responsible not only for the central bank's annual lending plans but also for the implementation by various branches in order to control money circulation and the size of credit generated by the People's Bank of China. The credit plans of national banks included the capital sources and uses of the People's Bank of China, state agency banks, state-owned commercial banks, the Bank of Communications, and postal savings agencies. The credit plans of other financial institutions mainly referred to the capital sources and uses by other commercial banks, credit cooperatives in both urban and rural areas, and various financial trust and investment companies. The credit activity plans for direct financing by enterprises referred to the size of corporate financing plans for the issuance of equities and bonds.

Although credit rationing by the People's Bank of China led to huge efficiency losses and was even gradually running out of control, the credit plan system played an important role in regulating the economy.

Meanwhile, as a direct regulation and control tool, credit size control and interest rate regulation had noticeable power and effects, which could easily cause economic fluctuations. It is safe to say that the credit plan was a powerful tool by which the People's Bank of China could manage the economy.

Before 1984 China controlled differential credit, which means that if one bank received more deposits or capital, it could issue more loans. However, at the end of 1984 the national credit plan conference proposed reforming the credit management system by basing credit on the prior year's loan balance starting with 1985 and each year thereafter. To obtain a higher loan base, almost all commercial banks competed with each other to expand lines of credit before the end of 1984, which increased the money supply by 49 percent versus the prior year, and credit was running out of control. Therefore, since 1985, the central bank had taken strict measures to reduce credit size, which led to economic slowdown in the second half of 1985 (see Figure 3.1, which covers the period from reform until the introduction of indirect regulation and controls).

The inflation rate decreased from 9.3 percent in 1985 to 6.5 percent in 1986, while the economic growth rate suddenly decreased from 13.5 percent in 1985 to 8.8 percent in 1986. In 1988, China started reforming the price system, which led to nationwide purchasing panic.

Figure 3.1 Chinese GDP Growth and Inflation Rates, 1978–1997

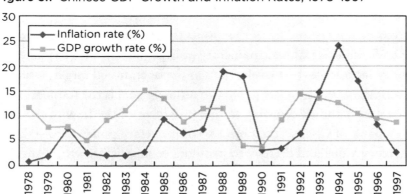

The inflation rate jumped from 7.3 percent in 1987 to 18.8 percent in 1988. In September 1988 the central government had to implement a highly contractionary monetary policy, causing the economic growth rate to slump from 11.3 percent in 1988 to 4.1 percent in 1989. With monetary policies taking effect from 1988 to 1991, the inflation rate returned to normal. In 1992, when Deng Xiaoping delivered a speech during the "southern tour," the economy took off and credit expanded quickly. As a result, the inflation rate reached double digits. Under such circumstances, the People's Bank of China did not cool the overheated economy with the same tight money policy as in the two previous periods. Instead, moderately tight monetary and fiscal policies were adopted, and the economy successfully realized a soft landing in 1996.

Since 1996 China had officially chosen the money supply as the intermediate target, and it declared goals for M1 money supply growth to average 18 percent and for M2 money supply growth to average 23 percent during the period of the Ninth Five-Year Plan. At the same time, the People's Bank of China officially used money supply as the intermediate target and issued supply targets for three types of money, namely M0, M1, and M2. With the development of a market economy, money supply quantity was no longer determined solely by money supply as in the past, but was more controlled by monetary demand, enhancing internal money supplies.

The Objective of the Chinese Monetary Policy: Ultimate Goal and Intermediate Target

Accurate understanding of the monetary policy's objective is the key to understanding Chinese monetary policy. The objective of monetary policy includes several levels, such as the operational target, intermediate target, and ultimate goal. The ultimate goal is the foundation of monetary policy. According to one provision of the Law of the People's Bank of China, "the objective of monetary policy is to stabilize currency value and thereby to promote economic growth." Another provision of the law states that "under the guidance of the State Council, the People's Bank of China formulates and implements monetary policies." Currently, as China is facing economic transformation as well as development, monetary policy becomes a part of the macroeconomic regulation and control system and often needs to balance four basic objectives—price stability, economic growth, full employment, and balance of international payments.

The Formulation of Monetary Policy Goals Varies

Generally speaking, the main objectives of monetary policy are price stability, economic growth, full employment, and balancing international payments. Since full employment is consistent with economic growth, price stability includes the stability of the domestic price and exchange rate, while exchange rate stability is related to balancing international payments. Therefore, the ultimate goal of monetary policy is currency stability and economic growth.

Due to differences in economic, political, geographical, and historical factors, economists have brought forth different views regarding the ultimate goal of monetary policy. The economists of the Keynesian school believe that monetary policy should achieve multiple goals, for they view the macroeconomy as chaotic and lacking in order, while monetarist economists believe that monetary policy should have a single goal because multiple goals usually cannot be achieved at the same time. At the beginning of the reform and opening up, the goal of China's monetary policy was to take both price stability and economic growth into consideration, which was consistent with the situation at that time to grow productivity. As a matter of fact, dual goals could hardly be fulfilled. As economic aggregate increased and the contradiction between supply and demand was alleviated, China changed its monetary policy objective to maintaining the stability of its currency to promote economic growth.

Based on execution of the Chinese monetary policy, the first-tier objective is to maintain currency stability, that is, maintaining basic domestic price stability and the stability of effective RMB exchange rates internationally. Since the reform and opening up, China has witnessed inflation for five periods and deflation during one period due to external factors. Therefore, inflation is normal and deflation is abnormal. Monetary policies always guard against inflation. For the time being, due to certain limitations on the CPI calculation method, the policy of macro regulation and control and monetary policy should take both CPI (consumer price index) and PPI (producer price index) into account (see Figure 3.2). Consideration should also be given to the price of assets, such as real estate and equity, as well as the expectation of consumer prices. The RMB effective exchange rate refers to both the nominal effective exchange rate and actual effective exchange rate. According to statistics, the nominal effective exchange rate is useful in the short run, whereas the actual effective exchange rate is useful in the middle and long run. So far, China has basically completed its reform on the mechanism of setting the RMB exchange rate to meet the objective of maintaining the basic stability of RMB at a rational and balanced level in accordance with the framework of "allowing exchange rates to be determined by market supply and demand, referencing exchange rates to a basket of currencies and managing exchange rates on a floating rate basis."

Figure 3.2 Chinese CPI and PPI Trend, 1999–2009

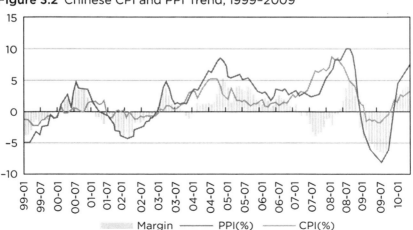

The second-tier objective of Chinese monetary policy is to promote economic growth and increase employment. Although promoting economic growth is an objective subordinated to currency value
stability, the attention paid to economic growth is no less than that
paid to price stability from the standpoint of implementing monetary
policy. For example, the fixed quantity of the economic growth target
was mentioned in the Five-Year Plan that stipulated China's middle-
term economic growth, the annual *Government Work Report*, and the
Report on Monetary Policy Implementation. In recent years, China's
GDP was growing at a rate of approximately 10 percent. Even during the period 2008–2009 when the world was hit hard by the financial crisis, the Chinese economic growth rate still exceeded 9 percent
(see Figure 3.3).

The Intermediate Target of the Monetary Policy

Because there is a time lag from the initiation of monetary tools to
their impact on economic growth and price stability, which are ultimate goals that monetary authorities are concerned about, monetary
authorities of all nations usually adopt the so-called intermediate target to achieve policy objectives. The intermediate target of monetary

Figure 3.3 Chinese GDP Aggregate and Growth Rate, 1978–2009

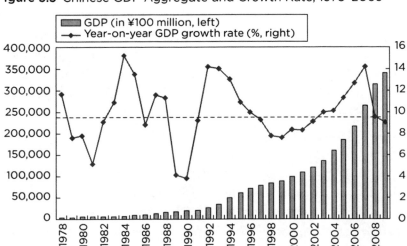

policy is an observable and adjustable index set by the central bank, a financial variable that will lead to the ultimate fulfillment of monetary policy objectives. The intermediate target primarily includes the quantity of money supply and interest rates. Whether the intermediate target should be money supply quantity or interest rates has been a classic topic of heated discussions in both monetary policy theory and practice. The choice should be based on which of the targets will be more closely related to economic growth and price stability, as well as whether it is the industrial sector or the financial sector that impacts the economy.

In general, the variable that acts as the intermediate target of monetary policy should have the characteristics of controllability, predictability, and relevance. Controllability refers to the ability of a central bank to regulate and control target financial variables by means of various monetary policy tools. Predictability refers to the ability of a central bank to gain prompt and accurate access to information on target variables. Relevance is the correlation between the intermediate target or the operational target and the ultimate goal. If there is high correlation, the central bank can achieve the ultimate goal of monetary policy by accurately controlling the intermediate target. Of course, the intermediate target of monetary policy is constantly changing and usually relies on the execution mechanism of a central bank's monetary policy, varying with different countries at different times (see Table 3.2).

In recent years, the establishment and improvement of the monetary policy intermediate target system became a major milestone during the reform of the Chinese currency regulation mechanism, manifested by the termination of controls over commercial banks' lending capacity, the establishment of the operational target based on monetary base and the intermediate target based on money supply quantity, and significant progress on market-oriented interest rate reforms.

With regard to actual monetary policy implementation, China published money supply volumes in 1993 for the first time and then in 1996 adopted money supply M1 and M2 (Figure 3.4) as the control target, which further confirmed that the money supply had been established as the intermediate target.

Table 3.2 The Evolution of the Post–WWII Monetary Policy
Objectives of Major Developed Countries

	1950s–1960s	1970s–1980s	After 1990
Economic background	After economic recession, unemployment was a very serious issue.	Economy slumped into stagnation.	Economy began to recover but inflation was high.
Theoretical basis of monetary policy	Keynesian theory emphasized fiscal policy.	Monetarism focused on monetary policy.	Emphasis was on the coordination between monetary policy and fiscal policy.
The ultimate goal of monetary policy	Full employment and economic growth were the main goal.	Price stability was the main goal.	Anti-inflation was the main goal.
The intermediate target of monetary policy	Interest rate was the intermediate target.	Money supply quantity was the intermediate target.	Abolishing money supply quantity was the intermediate target.
The operational target of monetary policy	Short-term interest rates, interbank borrowing market interest rates and the level of reserves were main operational targets.		

Figure 3.4 Chinese Money Supply, 2001–2009

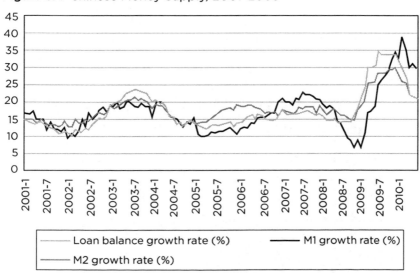

Loan balance growth rate (%)   M1 growth rate (%)
M2 growth rate (%)

China's monetary policy began to transform from direct regulation and control to indirect regulation and control, marked by the termination of mandatory credit quantity planning on January 1, 1998. But the transformation did not change the pattern of focusing on quantity regulation and control. It simply replaced credit quantity with money supply quantity as the monetary policy's intermediate target and changed the target from the asset to the liability of financial institutions. As financial institutions increased diversification and the percentage of foreign exchange assets in their portfolios, it would be incomplete to focus only on the credit, for the broad money supply (M2) was a comprehensive indicator of aggregate demand and currency.

With the development of the money market and the improvement of financial institutions' pricing power and internal management capabilities, market entities were more and more sensitive to interest rates as well as the influence of interest rates on the financial market and market participants. Meanwhile, the exchange rate reform and the adjustments of and expectations on exchange rates were having a greater influence on financial institutions, the financial market, and consumer behavior. Under such circumstances, besides indirect quantitative controls, monetary policy should also give due consideration to the price target. In summary, the implementation of the Chinese monetary policy was to align the relationships between the quantity target and price target, liquidity and market interest rates, market interest rates and official interest rates, and interest rates and exchange rates.

Chinese Monetary Policy: Policy Instruments and Execution Mechanism

Monetary policy instruments, including common and optional monetary policy instruments and direct and indirect credit control instruments, are used by the central bank to achieve monetary policy objectives. Specifically, common monetary policy instruments include the official deposit reserve ratio, discount loan and discount rate, and open market operations. Optional monetary policy instruments can be categorized into controls on consumer credit, controls on fixed-asset loans, and controls on security market borrowings. Direct credit control instruments consist of the credit allocation, direct intervention, liquidity ratio, and maximum limit on interest rates. Indirect credit control instruments mainly consist of moral persuasion and window guidance. According to relevant provisions of the Law of the People's Bank of China, China's monetary policy instruments are mainly composed of the deposit reserve, central bank reference rate, discount rate, central bank lending, open market operations, and other monetary policy instruments stipulated by the State Council.

With continuing reforms on the Chinese financial system, it has been a fundamental principle for the monetary policy operations to flexibly apply various market-oriented instruments. Relying on the basic financial system dominated by banks, the interbank market is gradually becoming the most important short-term financing source for financial institutions and a platform for the central bank's monetary policy operations. At present, the central bank's monetary policy has mainly four quantitative instruments and two price instruments. The former include open market operations, the deposit reserve, relending and discounting, and credit plan guidance and window guidance; the latter consist of the interest rate and exchange rate (see Table 3.3). All of the six monetary policy instruments are market oriented. Flexible coordination and application of these instruments is critical to the success of monetary policy. It is not surprising for China to use any of these six instruments to fulfill monetary policy objectives according to the actual needs of macroeconomic regulation and control.

In recent years, the main task of monetary policy has been to maintain price stability and exchange rate stability, provided that both the current account and capital account have surpluses. As to policy execution, to maintain the stability of the RMB exchange rate the central bank had to buy in the foreign exchange market all foreign

Table 3.3 Chinese Monetary Policy Instruments

Instruments	Features	Illustration
Open market operations	The most commonly used and the most flexible instrument	China's open market operations began in 1996 and played a more and more important role in hedging excess liquidity due to the purchase of excessive foreign exchange. By March 2010, the balance of securities issued by the central bank has reached 4.73 trillion yuan.
Deposit reserve ratio	Instrument with a major role during special periods	As one of the three traditional monetary policy instruments, the deposit reserve ratio is usually used in conjunction with open market operations during a special period (e.g., 2003–2007) of overheated economy and excessive monetary credit in order to control excess liquidity. When the economy is in recession, the central bank reduces the deposit reserve ratio according to the actual conditions to increase credit availability.
Relending/ discounting	Instrument focused on reducing the money supply	Generally speaking, relending and discounting are intended to reduce the money supply in consideration of the overall situation. Relending can be flexibly structured and increased or decreased as needed. For instance, the policy of relending to rural credit cooperatives in support of agriculture is very flexible and provides support to rural the economy.
Instructive credit plans/ window guidance	Auxiliary instrument	Credit is a major source of the money supply. When the economy is overheated, window guidance is helpful to bringing the credit market back to normal. At present, market instruments are considered a priority, supplemented with instructive plans and window guidance, which play a timely and effective role in the execution of monetary policy.

exchange that flowed into China under these two accounts and meanwhile sell RMB. In order to maintain price stability, the central bank must control money supply quantity to balance money supply with demand. When foreign exchange inflows were low, the exchange rate

Table 3.3 Chinese Monetary Policy Instruments (continued)

Instruments	Features	Illustration
Interest rates	Main instrument for indirect regulation and control	Currently, interest rate reform has achieved the periodic goal of setting ceilings for deposit rates and floors for lending rates. Combining international experience with Chinese actual conditions, China gradually tightens controls on the interest rate and its implementation and moves in the direction of gradual transformation from direct control on quantity to indirect control on prices (i.e., interest rates).
Exchange rates	Main instrument for indirect regulation	With the establishment of the managed floating exchange rate mechanism based on market demand and supply and the value of a basket of currencies, China has taken a decisive step in the reform of exchange rates. In the foreseeable future, the exchange rate mechanism will maintain relative stability and the market will play the most important role.

and consumer price stabilities could easily be reached simultaneously. However, when foreign exchange inflows were large, the central bank was compelled to release an excessive amount of RMB in the process of buying foreign exchange, which might lead to conflicts between exchange rate stability and price stability.

To solve the problem brought about by the constant inflows of foreign exchange, the central bank used monetary policy instruments to offset excessive money supply increases due to continuous purchase of foreign exchange under the established exchange rate policy to maintain price stability. Figure 3.5 shows three stages starting from 2000 in which the central bank used monetary policy instruments to offset money supply increases. The first stage ended in August 2002 when the increase of foreign assets slowed down and offsetting instruments were unnecessary. The second stage started in September 2002 and ended in August 2006. Since the accumulation of foreign assets

Figure 3.5 Balancing Operations by the Central Bank: Bond Issuance and Deposit Reserve

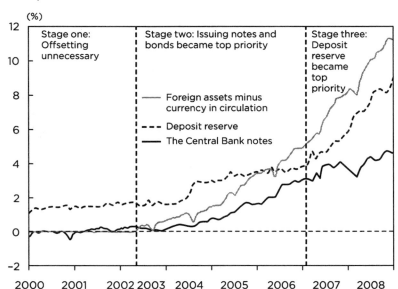

exceeded the growth of currency in circulation, the central bank began to reduce excessive liquidity by issuing central bank securities. By the end of August 2006, the securities issued by the central bank reached 2.9 trillion yuan, which accounted for 53 percent of the foreign asset increase during the same period. The third stage started in the second half of 2006. As foreign assets continued to grow, in addition to issuing securities the central bank increased the deposit reserve ratio to absorb excessive liquidity. During this period, the deposit reserve ratio was raised from 8 to 17.5 percent. Besides directly controlling money supply quantities by means of the above-mentioned quantitative instruments, the People's Bank of China also adjusted the benchmark interest rates for deposits and loans multiple times, as well as regulating and controlling the money supply through other price instruments.

The implementation of China's monetary policy clearly shows that the central bank flexibly adopted monetary policy instruments or a combination of instruments according to economic development. The most commonly used instruments were securities issued by the central bank, the deposit reserve ratio, and the benchmark interest rate. Issuing the central bank's securities can directly withdraw currency from circulation and decrease the supply of monetary base. Raising the deposit reserve ratio can restrict banks' lending capabilities, lower the money multiplier effect, and limit the increase of M2 money. Increasing the benchmark interest rate can directly regulate the value of capital and decrease the demand for money. Which instrument or instrument combination is to be adopted depends on the actual conditions of the economic development and the required objectives of macroeconomic regulation and control.

The Monetary Policy Execution Mechanism

The monetary policy's execution mechanism refers to the process of a central bank using monetary instruments in accordance with monetary policy objectives to affect manufacturing, investment, and consumption through the activities of financial institutions, enterprises, and consumers that are influenced by the financial market. In general, monetary policy execution is achieved through credit, interest rates, exchange rates, and asset prices. The execution of monetary policy generally involves market participants such as the central bank, financial markets, financial institutions, enterprises, and consumers.

Before the reform and opening up, commercial banks and the financial market did not exist in the planned economy in China. The monetary policy execution mechanism was direct and simple, basically following the execution path from the *People's Bank of China* to *branches of the People's Bank of China* to *enterprises*. Monetary policy fulfilled its ultimate goals by means of administrative orders. After the reform and opening up in the 1980s, with the establishment of the central bank system and the development of financial institutions, China gradually developed the central bank monetary policy execution mechanism, following the path from the *central bank → financial institutions → enterprises*. But the money market did not completely show up in the path. After the 1990s, with the transformation of macroeconomic control and further development of the money market, the mechanism of the *central bank → money market → financial institutions → enterprises* came into being, and the indirect execution mechanism of *policy instruments* to *operation target* to *intermediate target* to *ultimate goal* was also established.

During the development of Chinese monetary policy, 1998 was a critical year. Before 1998 Chinese monetary policy almost completely relied on the credit execution mechanism to regulate and control the economy. In comparison, the effect of the interest rate execution mechanism was weak, and the effect of the asset price and exchange rate was even weaker in the execution of monetary policy. Before this period, although the central bank system had been established and financial institutions, especially commercial banks, grew rapidly, the money market did not play any role in the execution process. Therefore, the execution of monetary policy followed the main line of *central bank → financial institutions → enterprises*. Later during this period, as the money market developed, its effect could no longer be ignored in the monetary policy execution mechanism, and the execution mechanism finally followed the line of *central bank → money market → financial institutions* to *enterprises*.

After 1998 the Chinese government actively promoted the reform of the monetary policy operation system. First, credit quantity control was lifted to increase the vitality of financial institutions and to promote the reform of the deposit reserve system. Second, interest rate reform was carried out steadily to accelerate interest rate marketization. Third, the money market was formed to increase the efficiency of the financial market. Fourth, reform of the interest rate formation mechanism and RMB convertibility for current account transactions were pursued, and the capital account opening proceeded with a steady and orderly pace. On that basis, China's monetary policy had basically achieved the transformation from direct control to indirect control, which fully demonstrated the execution mechanism to be *central bank → money market → financial institutions → enterprises*. The periodic development of the Chinese monetary policy execution mechanism can be summarized in Table 3.4.

Table 3.4 China's Monetary Policy Execution Mechanism in Different Stages

Policy instruments		Thirty years before the reform and opening up (1948–1978)	Twenty years after the reform and opening up (1979–1997)	Period of indirect regulation (after 1998)	Execution process
Policy instruments	Main instruments	Credit and cash plans	Credit and cash plans; Central bank loans	Central bank loans; Interest rate policies; Open market operations	→
	Auxiliary instruments	Credit policies; Interest rate policies; Administrative means	Interest rate policies; Credit policies; Discount; Open market operations; Special deposits	Deposit reserves; Discount; Instructive credit plans; Credit policies; Window guidance	
Operational target			Credit quantity transitioning to monetary base	Monetary base (monitoring liquidity)	
Immediate target		Four types of balances	Credit quantity transitioning to money supply	Money supply (monitoring the interest rate and exchange rate)	
Ultimate goal		Economic growth and stability of the consumer price	Economic growth and price stability, transitioning to economic growth with stable currency value	Economic growth with stable currency value	

Source: Yi Gang, The Framework of Chinese Monetary Policy.

The historic development of Chinese monetary policy practice reveals that the execution mechanism of Chinese monetary policy has undergone the transformation from administrative orders to market forces in accordance with the transformation from the centrally planned economy to a market economy. The core transformation is from direct control to indirect control. In a financial system dominated by banks, with financial institutions serving as intermediate links for monetary policy execution, reforming and developing commercial banks is critical to the execution mechanism of Chinese monetary policy.

During the period of direct regulation and control, the financial market did not participate in monetary policy execution. The credit activity of commercial banks was directly regulated and controlled by the central bank. There were explicit instructions and mandatory plans to determine the quantity of loans and the recipients of the loans. Due to defective controls over commercial banks, reckless investment was common. With further reforms on financial institutions since the 1990s, China made further progress in managing commercial banks and significantly improved their managerial capabilities. The successful reform on commercial banks was conducive to allowing the market to play its role and further strengthening the monetary policy execution mechanism. Especially when interest rate marketization moved forward steadily and financial institutions made progress in mastering pricing abilities and setting up the pricing system, monetary policy ushered in a new period of indirect regulation and control.

Under indirect regulation and control, the interest rate played a critical role in the monetary policy execution mechanism. Before the establishment of the Chinese indirect regulation and control system, the money market, capital market, and foreign exchange market were not fully developed because of strict controls over the interest rate and exchange rate. The central government implemented monetary policies by means of credit and cash plans. With bank deposits gradually increasing, bank loans increased and investment and consumption followed suit, which ultimately led to an increase in output. The execution mechanism is illustrated in Figure 3.6.

Figure 3.6 The Execution Mechanism of Chinese Monetary Policy

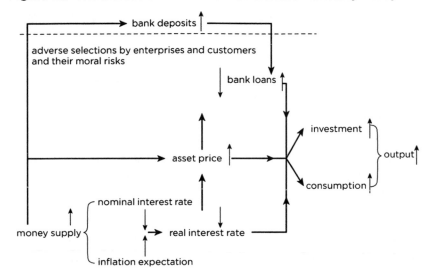

With the development of the financial market and the deregulation of the interest rate, the Chinese monetary policy execution mechanism began to align with the execution mechanism of the market economy. In terms of the interest rate execution mechanism, as the money supply increased, causing the nominal interest rate to decrease and inflation expectations to increase, the real interest rate dropped, which stimulated additional investment and consumption. As a result, output increased. With respect to the asset price execution mechanism, monetary expansion caused the prices of assets held by enterprises and consumers to increase, which led to further expansion of investment and the consumption propensity. Of course, since controls over foreign exchange still exist at present and RMB is freely convertible only under the current account, monetary policy cannot directly affect exchange rates or import and export through real interest rate changes.

Of course, the execution mechanism of Chinese monetary policy is not as simple as a few scratches shown in Figure 3.6. It is an interactive and complicated mechanism. Monetary policy execution is a complicated process that involves the central bank, the financial market, enterprises, and consumers and is not a result of one factor or one field. In addition, since the execution mechanism relies on such elements of the economic environment as economy of scale, market-oriented interest rate, borrowing and lending quantities, the objects and subjects in the financial system, financial structures and systems, macro expectations and financial services, and technology, it is very dynamic, varying with different time and locations.

As for the next stage of the reform, it will be critical for the monetary policy execution mechanism to further improve the mechanism for setting interest rates by commercial banks. With the development of the financial market and further opening of financing, the environmental changes brought about by the fluctuations of asset prices and financial innovations will definitely affect the Chinese monetary policy execution mechanism. Therefore, it will be necessary for China to proceed steadfastly with financial restructuring, further improve the development and transparency of the financial market, and do more research on the influences of financial innovations on the monetary policy execution mechanism in order to increase the efficiency of monetary policy execution.

The Future of Chinese Monetary Policy: Process and Trend

In the past 10 years, although China encountered a complex domestic and international economic environment, it constantly tried to improve its monetary policies. With multiple objectives in many actual scenarios, China did its utmost to consider the dual needs for reform and development when formulating monetary policies. While China proactively supported economic growth and restructuring, it also paid close attention to the overall stability of consumer prices to avoid dramatic economic fluctuations. Using various monetary policy instruments as well as a combination of monetary policy instruments, term structure, and enforcement, China was able to further improve monetary policies in terms of flexibility, efficiency, and effectiveness.

For the next stage, the main task of Chinese monetary policy is to further improve and consolidate the current system and actively study how to regulate the monetary policy system so as to make necessary adjustments to monetary policies to meet the needs of sustained economic growth in accordance with the changes of the internal and external environment. The following three aspects illustrate how China will further improve the monetary policy system.

First, the statutory goal of stabilizing currency value to generate economic growth should be further confirmed. In a relatively long period of time, as a large transitioning economy, China will have to direct monetary policies primarily to generate economic growth while keeping an eye on inflation. The monetary policy that focuses on economic growth is the product of the traditional planned economy under which the economy was led by the state and economic growth was driven by investments. With the establishment of China's market economy, the Law of the People's Bank of China passed in 1995 explicitly stipulates that the statutory goal of monetary policy is to maintain the stability of currency value to generate economic growth, thus officially recognizing the control over inflation as a top priority and a fundamental task. To execute monetary policies in the future, it is necessary for China to focus on the statutory goal to effectively control inflation expectations, deal with asset bubbles, and transform the economic development model. Especially in the event that RMB becomes a more important international currency, the stability of RMB value will help stabilize market expectations and improve the creditability of RMB as an international currency. In addition, as asset bubbles tend to trigger global financial crises, China has begun to actively explore monetary policies in search of a way to prevent systematic risks brought about by asset bubbles.

Second, monetary policy instruments will be transformed from quantity based to price based. In a transitioning economy, due to influences from the execution mechanism and policy directions, policy makers tend to focus on quantity-based instruments and avoid price-based instruments. This reflects the mentality of the traditional planned economy. With the overall establishment of the Chinese market economy and development of financial reforms, the influence of the price mechanism on the microeconomy is becoming more obvious, and it is more common to regulate the economy by means of price instruments. In recent years, the central bank began to pay attention to the use of price instruments. For example, potential inflation pressures were dealt with through the regulation of relending and discount rates. It is foreseeable that further consolidation and improvement as well as the deepening of China's financial market will prompt the transformation of quantity-based monetary policy instruments to price-based ones.

Third, the monetary policy execution mechanism will be further improved to build an effective financial environment. With the development of economic reforms, the financial institution operational goal is gradually changed to maximizing profits. However, compared with developed market economies, China still has a long way to go. Due to systematic factors, some microeconomic entities do not pursue profit maximization in financial activities, reducing the effectiveness of price-based monetary policy instruments. In recent years, in order to establish a microeconomy responsive to price signals, China began to strengthen corporate governance and the regulation and reform of financial institutions to improve the financial market conducive to effective monetary policy execution. It can be predicted that as the market economy develops and monetary policy turns its focus from direct to indirect control, the microeconomic foundation for monetary policy execution and the monetary policy execution mechanism will be greatly enhanced.

It should be pointed out that although the basic framework of China's future monetary policy has been based on the above three aspects, implementing monetary policy will be more difficult with the opening of the financial system in a new global environment. For example, as the capital account is opened up, capital flows are increasing significantly and the independence of monetary policy will be affected according to the classical theory of the Impossible Trinity.

What's more, the development of the stock market and electronic currency poses a significant challenge to the mass credit environment and currency circulation velocity. It is also a challenge for monetary policies to assess and deal with these changes.

CHAPTER 4

THE RMB EXCHANGE RATE

Chinese exchange rate reform will be based on the principles of autonomy, controllability, and progressiveness.

The objectives of the reform are to establish a managed floating exchange rate based on market supply and demand and to keep the RMB exchange rate relatively stable at a proper and balanced level.

Since July 2005, overall RMB appreciation has exceeded 20 percent.

China has never ceased to seek a reasonable equilibrium RMB exchange rate.

Exchange rates have always been a hot topic in economics, and related theories have been the center of international finance. Every country, no matter whether issuing its own currency or belonging to a monetary union, has a price of its currency represented in terms of a foreign currency, which is the so-called foreign exchange rate. Thus, studies concerning exchange rates have been considered one of the most challenging subjects. As a key economic variable in an open economy, the exchange rate is not only directly related to the current account and capital account but also a key factor influencing macroeconomic trends, since exchange rate fluctuations affect the profits and losses of foreign exchange trading organizations, and more importantly they affect a country's international trade, capital flows, consumer prices, and employment. There are two types of exchange rates, the real effective exchange rate and the nominal effective exchange rate. From the perspective of economic theories, the indicator that can best represent international price differences is the real effective exchange rate (REER), which not only reflects changes in dollars and the cross rate of other major currencies in the world but also adjusts for inflation differences between countries. But in reality, the nominal effective exchange rate that is not adjusted for inflation differences is more frequently used, because it is rather difficult to determine the adjustment factor for the real effective exchange rate, that is, the indicator of comparable prices of different countries.[1] Besides, the calculation of the real effective exchange rate is likely to be restricted by time lag and the availability of data.[2]

Exchange Rate and Exchange Rate System

The exchange rate, also called the conversion rate, is the ratio of a country's or region's currency to another country's or region's currency. In other words, it is a price of a currency in terms of another currency. The exchange rate is an important leverage in international trade. The costs of goods produced or sold in a certain country or region are calculated by local currency, and the prices and the competitiveness of these goods in the international market are directly affected by the exchange rate. The exchange rate can be either fixed or floating. Which exchange rate is better depends on the effectiveness of monetary policies and a country's economic strength, and different circumstances require a different exchange rate system.

RMB Exchange Rate Quotes and Transactions

The RMB exchange rate mainly depends on the supply and demand of the foreign exchange market. Every day, the People's Bank of China uses the previous day's closing price in the domestic foreign exchange market as well as the change of exchange rates of major currencies in the foreign financial markets to announce the exchange rate of RMB against the dollar and other major currencies. Banks or other financial institutions that are designated to conduct foreign exchange operations determine their own nominal exchange rates to transact with their clients based on exchange rates published by the central bank. In order to keep the nominal rate of each bank relatively consistent and stable, the People's Bank of China conducts open market operations through buying or selling foreign exchange at appropriate times in the interbank foreign exchange market.

The RMB exchange rate uses a direct quote. In the exchange rate quote list, foreign currencies are generally denominated in 100 units, with the exception of Belgian franc and Italian lira, which are denominated in 10,000, and Japanese yen, which is denominated in 100,000. The same rate applies when selling foreign exchange using wire transfer, mail transfer, or demand draft. At present, there are more than 20 exchange rates of RMB against foreign currencies (see examples in Figure 4.1 for the U.S. dollar, Great Britain pound, euro, and Japanese yen).

Banks designated with foreign currency transactions quote a bid price and an offer price when offering exchange rates, and the bid-ask spread equals 0.5 percent. In addition, there are also bid and ask quotes for foreign currencies in cash. The bid price for foreign currency in cash is usually 0.2 to 0.3 percent lower than the bid price for foreign exchange, but the offer price for cash is the same as that for foreign exchange.

The Bank of China started the business of forward RMB transactions in 1971 to meet the need for settling international trades using RMB. There are 15 foreign currencies that are qualified for forward transactions in exchange for RMB. The forward exchange rate in terms of RMB is quoted, not at par with or at a premium or discount to the spot rate, but by adding certain forward charges to the spot rate. There are six forward RMB delivery contracts, that is one month, two months, three months, four months, five months, and six months respectively.

The Influences of the RMB Exchange Rate on the Economy

As globalization continues to accelerate and China is becoming increasingly open to the world, exports become the important impetus for China's economic growth, and thus the exchange rate of RMB

Figure 4.1 The Exchange Rate of RMB Against USD, GBP, EURO, and JPY

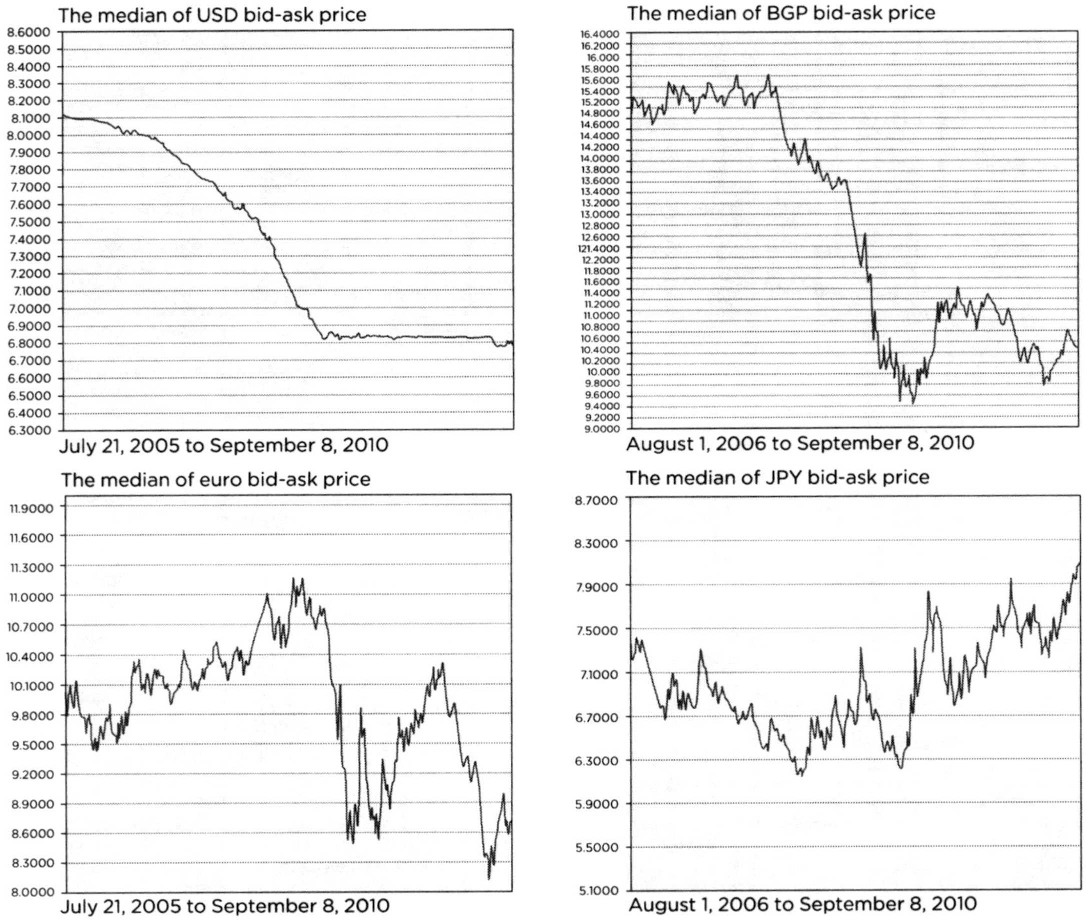

The median of USD bid-ask price

July 21, 2005 to September 8, 2010

The median of BGP bid-ask price

August 1, 2006 to September 8, 2010

The median of euro bid-ask price

July 21, 2005 to September 8, 2010

The median of JPY bid-ask price

August 1, 2006 to September 8, 2010

becomes more and more significant to internal and external economic equilibrium. The suffering from the depreciation of RMB due to the 1997 Asian financial crisis was not long before the appreciation of RMB quickly became an issue to haunt China. While people still had fresh memories of the exchange rate reform on July 21, 2005, some already suggested currency depreciation shortly afterward. Therefore, China urgently needs to answer the following questions: what exchange rate system is most appropriate for RMB, where is the equilibrium point, and how will the fluctuations of the RMB exchange rate affect Chinese and world economic growth?

Exchange rates keep changing under different circumstances. The changes have significant influences on trade, investment, and even economic growth at home and abroad. Since China is a rapidly growing, emerging economy, it is obvious that the changes in China's exchange rate will affect the economies of trade counterparties and even the whole world. Take the influences of RMB appreciation on the domestic economy as an example. Positive influences include enhanced international purchasing power, lowered pressures from foreign borrowings, strengthened foreign investment ability, and lowered costs for some domestic enterprises, while negative influences include lowered exports and foreign investments, increased pressures from deflation, and damages to enterprises that simply rely on price advantages to compete in the marketplace.

As a matter of fact, the exchange rate not only affects international trade and global economic balance from the external perspective and domestic economic growth and restructuring from the internal perspective; it is also closely related to international capital flows and monetary policies. According to the Impossible Trinity in international finance, an open economy cannot pursue all of these three aspects: stable exchange rates, free capital flows, and independent monetary policies. Generally only two of the aspects can be realized simultaneously. As a country with a population of 1.3 billion, in order to strengthen the independence of the government in controlling the economy, China will certainly not give up its independent monetary policies. As a result, the exchange rate of RMB and relevant policies are key issues that are closely related to China's long-term economic development.

The Administration of the Exchange Rate

In China, foreign exchange administration and policy making are the responsibilities of the State Administration of Foreign Exchange (SAFE). The policy making mainly refers to determining the level of exchange rates and the specific aspects of rate changes, including determining the timing of changes, creating necessary conditions, applying procedures, methods, and measures, and so on.

Just as China transformed from a planned economy to a market economy, the SAFE also experienced enormous changes. In March 1979 the State Council approved setting up the State General Administration of Foreign Exchange to manage the nation's foreign exchange revenues and payments. In August 1982, in accordance with the principle of separating government functions from managing enterprises, the General Administration was merged into the People's Bank of China. Its name was changed to the State Administration of Foreign Exchange and it exclusively exercised the power of administering foreign exchange. In 1988 it was again assigned directly to the State Council and was temporarily supervised by the People's Bank of China.

The major responsibilities of the SAFE are as follows: (1) to draw up guidelines, policies, laws, regulations, and rules of foreign exchange administration and put all of these into practice; (2) to participate in the planning of the state's foreign exchange revenues and payments and the planning of foreign capital usage, and to lead statistical reporting of balance of international payments and prepare the statements of balance of international payments; (3) to draft policies and operating principles for national foreign exchange reserves and manage the reserves on behalf of the People's Bank of China; (4) to draw up policies for the exchange rate of RMB and supervise the foreign exchange market; (5) to be responsible for foreign debt registration and management of short-term foreign borrowings; (6) to be responsible for approving and supervising the foreign exchange operations of financial institutions; and (7) to inspect and deal with activities that violate foreign exchange regulations.

Before 1994 the exchange rate of RMB was determined and published by the SAFE. But since the unification of RMB exchange rates on January 1, 1994, a single, managed floating exchange rate system based on market supply and demand has been established. The People's Bank of China announces the exchange rate of RMB against the dollar and other major currencies every day, according to the prior day's transaction prices from the interbank foreign exchange market. On that basis, each bank autonomously determines its daily trading prices within the floating range allowed by the People's Bank of China.

The Equilibrium Exchange Rate of RMB: An Economic Puzzle Still Unresolved

There are numerous theories on exchange rates and hot debates exist concerning how to calculate the equilibrium exchange rate of RMB. To solve the puzzle of the equilibrium exchange rate of RMB, we have to look at the exchange rate system. Only then can we reveal the true "answer" to the equilibrium exchange rate.

Theoretically, each exchange rate theory has its own calculation method. Unfortunately, there is no definitive conclusion as to which method is better. Domestic and foreign authoritative institutions, that is, the SAFE, the International Monetary Fund (IMF), the World Bank, and the European Central Bank mentioned in this chapter, and economists at home and abroad, draw different conclusions with regard to the equilibrium RMB exchange rate. Authoritative institutions often utilize the PPP (purchasing power parity) model but rarely any modern exchange rate theories, while academics utilize all sorts of exchange rate theories to do the calculation.[3] Various authorities use different calculating methods. The SAFE calculates and publishes the RMB middle rate, the IMF regularly issues the RMB real exchange rate index, the World Bank does not calculate the RMB exchange rate but discusses the RMB exchange rate in its quarterly Chinese economic reviews, the Bank for International Settlements (BIS) publishes China's official exchange rate, and the European Central Bank only states its opinions without calculating the RMB exchange rate.

Before the opening of the interbank foreign exchange market each day, the SAFE solicits quotes from dealers, selects the median of the USD exchange rate quote from each dealer, and discards the highest and the lowest quotes to calculate a weighted average exchange rate for RMB against the U.S. dollar, which becomes the median of the official bid and ask price for the day. The weight in this calculation is determined by the China Foreign Exchange Trade System in accordance with each dealer's trade volume and prices in the interbank foreign exchange market. The China Foreign Exchange Trade System also calculates the middle rates for RMB against the euro, JPY, HKD (Hong Kong), and GBP, which are based on the middle rate of RMB against USD for the day and the exchange rates for the U.S. dollar against the euro, JPY, HKD, and GBP in the international foreign exchange rate market at 9 a.m. on the same day.

Various theoretical methods come up with various equilibrium RMB exchange rates, let alone that these calculation methods are controversial themselves. While some scholars believe RMB has been undervalued to a certain degree, other top researchers in this field, such as McKinnon (2004), strongly believe that the current RMB exchange rate is at its best level. Generally speaking, looking at exchange rate theories and actuality, we cannot find a theory for predicting the exchange rate that is able to match the actual rate with high consistency. This is an important reason why most nations do not simply rely on theoretical calculations to determine their exchange rates.

Economic theories hold that various exchange rate systems have their advantages and disadvantages, and affect economies in different ways. When selecting an exchange rate system, a nation must consider a series of issues, such as the independence of monetary policy, international trade, and inflation. Most research on RMB exchange rates has been focusing on structural models and selection of input variables with a purpose of calculating equilibrium RMB exchange rates. However, the divergences of results from large, convoluted calculations demonstrate that simply using modern exchange rate theories and predetermined views to select input variables and methods will not lead to conclusive results. As a matter of fact, the choice of the exchange rate system is subject to many noneconomic factors, such as political power in the international arena, interference from special interest groups, and cultural traditions.

Similarly, the current reform of the RMB exchange rate will first of all consider political and economic restrictions. The Chinese banking industry started a painful reform in 1997. Even though it successfully segregated nonperforming loans and raised capital, the banking system is still vulnerable, lacking in innovations and operational experience related to the interest rate and exchange rate. Complete removal of exchange rate restrictions will probably cause damages. If the banking system were in danger of collapsing, the central bank would likely be forced to issue currency to cover losses of the banking industry, causing systemic chaos to the Chinese monetary system. With widespread market speculations and irrational expectations on RMB appreciation, expectations on RMB appreciation would jump each time that RMB appreciates less than expected, forcing the ultimate RMB exchange rate to deviate from equilibrium. China is still a developing market economy, and employment and economic growth is the top priority. The appreciation of the currency will have opposite effects, that is, lowered exports and employment.

During the transitioning process in China, a stable internal and external environment is critical to economic growth. Toward the end of the twentieth century the Chinese economy put on a spectacular performance that is primarily attributed to stability and development. While the unmanaged floating exchange rate system is more effective, the managed floating exchange rate system is more conducive to domestic economic stability. As the current Chinese financial system is still at its early stage, both financial institutions and manufacturing entities lack sufficient capabilities to deal with the constantly changing international financial market. Under this circumstance, China cannot simply rely on textbook conclusions or certain research data to determine equilibrium exchange rates; it needs to take many realistic factors, both domestic and international, into consideration.

The RMB Exchange Rate System: Historical Process and Evaluation

The exchange rate system (also called exchange rate arrangement) refers to a series of arrangements or regulations by the monetary authority of a certain country regarding issues such as the determination of the exchange rate level and ways of adjustments. Every nation adopts appropriate exchange rates according to particular conditions and makes necessary adjustments according to changes. The exchange rate system plays an important role in achieving the internal and external balance of a country's economy. Since the RMB exchange rate was first issued in 1949, it has experienced changes from the planned economy to the market economy, from the closed economy to the open economy, and from inflexibility to flexibility. In particular, since the reform and opening-up policy, the RMB exchange rate system reform has been further implemented. The changes of the RMB exchange rate cannot be accomplished with one stroke. The changes need to show the internal logic, directions, and principles of the exchange rate system, demonstrating that they have met the needs of economic development in different phases and gradually adopted international standards.

Changes of the RMB Exchange Rate System: 1949–2010

Since 1949 the RMB exchange rate system has evolved from an official rate system to a rate determined by the market, and from a fixed rate system to a managed floating rate system. From 1949 to the year of the reform and opening up, RMB exchange rates were under strict control by the state. In accordance with the needs of different periods, China's exchange rate has gone through the following three systems: a single floating exchange rate system (1949–1952), a single fixed exchange rate system (1953–1972), and a single floating exchange rate system with reference to a basket of foreign currencies (1973–1980).

After the Third Plenary Session of the Eleventh Central Committee, China started the transformation from a planned economy to a socialist market economy, ushering in a new stage for the reform and opening up. To encourage exports, China transformed from a single-rate system to a dual-rate system as exemplified by these two periods. From 1981 to 1984, the official exchange rate and internal settlement exchange rate for trades coexisted. From 1985 to 1993, the official exchange rate and the adjusted foreign exchange rate coexisted. During that period, the dual exchange rate system played an important role in balancing international payments and facilitating the central bank's control of the amount of currency in circulation. However, along with further reform and opening up, the coexistence of the official exchange rate and adjusted exchange rate increasingly demonstrated its drawbacks. The coexistence of multiple exchange rates brought disorders to the foreign exchange market and fostered speculation. In addition, foreign exchange was traded in the black market, which affected the stability of RMB and its credit.

In December 1993 China initiated foreign exchange reform with a decision to merge the official exchange rate and the adjusted exchange rate, established a unified managed floating exchange rate system based on market supply and demand, terminated the foreign exchange retention system, and implemented the system of purchasing and selling foreign exchange. On January 1, 1994, the official RMB exchange rate merged with the adjusted exchange rate, and a single managed floating exchange rate system based on market supply and demand came into effect in China (Figure 4.2). Enterprises and individuals traded foreign currencies with banks in accordance with relevant regulations, and banks traded with each other in the interbank foreign exchange market. The market set exchange rates. The central bank controlled the foreign exchange market and maintained the stability of the RMB exchange rate by setting a range within which foreign exchange was allowed to float.

Before 1997 the RMB exchange rate appreciated steadily, which increased confidence in RMB at home and abroad. When the Asian financial crisis broke out, China reduced the RMB exchange rate floating range to prevent the worsening of the crisis caused by further depreciation of currencies of neighbor countries and regions, and it began to peg RMB to the U.S. dollar. In 1999 the IMF considered RMB a currency pegged to the U.S. dollar.

Figure 4.2 Exchange Rate Reform in 1994

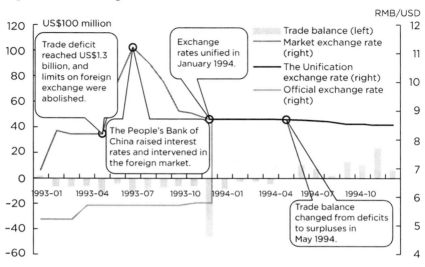

Source: People's Bank of China.

As the impact of the Asian financial crisis abated, China began to see sustained and steady economic development, gradual deepening of economic reforms, new achievements in the restructuring of the financial system, further relaxation of foreign exchange controls, and expansion of the foreign exchange market in scope and depth. All of these created favorable conditions for the improvement of the RMB exchange rate system.

On July 21, 2005, the People's Bank of China declared the RMB exchange rate reform, and that the RMB exchange rate will not peg to the value of a single currency, the U.S. dollar, but to a basket of foreign currencies in accordance with economic development. The RMB exchange rate immediately appreciated 2.1 percent against USD and the exchange rate was placed under a managed floating system with the daily fluctuation range to be 0.3 percent. Further reform proceeded on May 18, 2007, with a greater fluctuation range of 0.5 percent from May 21, 2007.

On June 19, 2010, the People's Bank of China announced further reforms to improve the RMB exchange rate setting. The reform would focus on the dynamic management and regulation of RMB rate fluctuations, referencing a basket of foreign currencies and preannounced exchange rate fluctuation intervals. Such effort would improve the managed floating exchange rate system and contribute to keeping the exchange rate relatively stable at a proper and balanced level, balancing international payments and enhancing financial market stability, and thereby achieving sustainable long-term economic growth.

The history of the RMB exchange rate reform is illustrated by Figure 4.3.

The Achievements and Experience from the Reform of the RMB Exchange Rate System

At the beginning, China planned that the reform would achieve a managed floating exchange rate truly based on market supply and demand. This system would basically contain the following aspects: (1) it would allow exchange rates to float based on market supply and demand and

Figure 4.3 The History of RMB Exchange Rate Reform

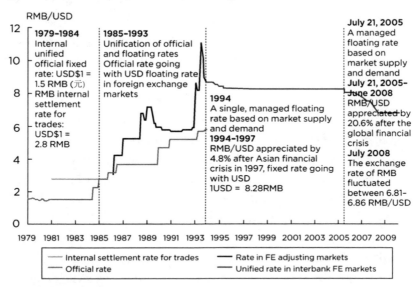

Source: People's Bank of China.

to play the role of price discovery; (2) it would utilize the advantage of "managed" floating to adjust floating ranges according to the current account activities, especially the balance of trade; (3) it would watch the value of a basket of foreign currencies rather than only pay attention to a specific foreign currency.

Based on the execution of the managed floating exchange rate system, it has met these three basic requirements, that is, "market supply and demand," "managed," and "floating." First, the reform was intended to authentically reflect market supply and demand. Having controllable risks, it gradually loosened control over foreign exchange; widened the control areas; encouraged more economic entities to voluntarily participate, thus reflecting market supply and demand as well as true trading intentions; and laid the foundation for the further market-oriented exchange rate system. Second, the reform applied a variety of methods, including direct intervention by the central bank in the foreign exchange market and comprehensive adjustments of the supply and demand of domestic and foreign currencies as well as interest rates. Third, the reform followed the principles of stability and progressiveness by gradually broadening the exchange rate floating range and increasing the flexibility of the RMB exchange rate (Figure 4.4).

In a word, as the reform has deepened, the managed floating exchange rate system has been greatly improved, which can be shown in the following aspects.

First, a more proper and balanced dynamic system has come into being. Since 1978 the RMB exchange rate has moved from depreciation to appreciation. RMB first depreciated from 1.5 RMB per dollar, and appreciated from 8.7 RMB per dollar in early 1994 to 8.11 RMB per dollar in 2005, and further to about 6.85 RMB per dollar in 2009 (see Figure 4.5). The floating range has been broadened, and the daily USD floating range was raised from 0.3 percent in 2005 to 0.5 percent in 2007. Market participants began to seek proper, balanced, and dynamic exchange rates using such factors as balance of international payments, the supply and demand of foreign exchange, and so on.

Figure 4.4 The RMB Exchange Rate Becomes More Flexible

Source: People's Bank of China.

Figure 4.5 Four Stages of RMB Exchange Rates Against USD After 2005 Reform

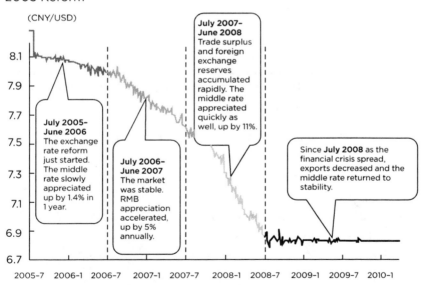

Source: People's Bank of China.

Second, the price of foreign exchange is dependent on the market supply and demand. At the end of 1996, foreign exchange under the current account became convertible. Since 2001 capital flows, including foreign direct investment, equity investment, and offshore financing, have increased, and the relationship between foreign exchange demand and supply has become more balanced. It has become more convenient for individuals to hold and use foreign exchange for international trade and investment. Therefore, the relationship of foreign exchange supply and demand has been fully reflected in the market.

Third, the market mechanism for the exchange rate has been improved. Before 1994 there was a dual exchange rate system in which the official rate and the adjusted rate existed simultaneously. It was transformed into a system that had quotes from foreign exchange market dealers and involved market makers. Afterward, the foreign exchange market grew rapidly, and market participants played a more and more important role in shaping up the middle rate. Due to diversified foreign trade and investment, exchange rates were gradually adjusted to consider a basket of foreign currencies rather than only the U.S. dollar.

The Features of the New Rate-Setting Mechanism of the RMB Exchange

- In a market economy, it is the market that basically allocates resources. As a result, the rate-setting mechanism of the RMB exchange rate should be based on market supply and demand, referencing a basket of foreign currencies.
- Because market adjustments are usually spontaneous and directionless with lagging effects, China must reinforce macroeconomic regulation and control by the state. In other words, the exchange rate should be managed.
- The mechanism is based on market supply and demand, referencing the value of a basket of foreign currencies. The government determines a range of RMB exchange rates. Therefore, RMB exchange rates should be floating.

RMB Exchange Rate Reform: Objectives, Principles, and Directions

Exchange rate reform is one of the important steps in completing the rate-setting mechanism for the RMB exchange rate. It is a significant element in reforming the economic and financial system and in establishing and improving the socialist market economy. It is beneficial to China in the long run, as it helps promote comprehensive, balanced, and sustainable economic and social development. Moreover, the reform will certainly and profoundly impact the economies of the Asian-Pacific areas and even the whole world.

Objectives

In accordance with the requirements of reforming the RMB exchange rate setting mechanism, the general objectives of the RMB exchange rate reform are to improve a managed floating exchange rate in accordance with market supply and demand and keep RMB relatively stable at a proper and balanced level. The reform will not necessarily emphasize a certain rate target. Instead, it is aimed at forming a mechanism that will enable the exchange rate to basically reflect market supply and demand and, more importantly, helping promote the balance of international payments.

Principles

The history of the exchange rate reform reflects the principles of market orientation, progressiveness, and independence, consistent with those of the Chinese economic reform and reflecting the necessity of transforming national development strategies.

First, the exchange rate reform is market orientated. At the beginning of the exchange rate reform, China determined that market orientation would be the direction of the reform. There were three aspects related to the changes of exchange rates: the determination of rate levels, the reference system of rate fluctuations, and the fluctuation range. From the establishment of the foreign exchange allocation market at the beginning of the reform and opening up till the establishment of the interbank foreign exchange market in 1994, the RMB exchange rate gradually moved toward a market-oriented system. In 1994 China clarified the reform of the exchange rate system to follow the direction of the market. As current account foreign exchange became fully convertible in 1996, the market mechanism played a more and more important role in setting the RMB exchange rate. Since the reform on July 21, 2005, while allowing the RMB exchange rate to fluctuate and appreciate by a small percentage, the People's Bank of China gradually reduced controls over the exchange rate and allowed the market to play its role, which enabled the foreign exchange market to spontaneously seek the equilibrium exchange rate.

Second, the exchange rate reform is progressive. The process of the reform is seen in the following stages. In the first stage (1979–1993), China applied foreign exchange planned allocation and market trading, and it adopted the combination of the official exchange rate and market exchange rate. The second stage started in 1994, when a single, managed floating exchange rate was adopted; later in 1996 the current account transactions became completely convertible. In the third stage, a managed floating exchange rate system based on market supply and demand, with reference to a basket of foreign currencies, was established in 2005. These stages clearly demonstrated the principles of the exchange rate reform. From the macroeconomic perspective, the exchange rate system in the planned economy before the reform and opening up was not suitable for a market economy, and the reform was inevitable. However, Chinese situations did not allow "shock therapy." Thus progressive exchange rate reform became a choice and was integrated into the overall economic reform. From the microeconomic perspective, the reason why China adopted a progressive reform was that it must take market changes into consideration as well as the tolerance of all stakeholders.

Third, the exchange rate reform is independent. Exchange rate system reform is closely related to a country's sovereignty, and every country is entitled to choose a system that is suitable for its conditions.

Under complicated domestic and international conditions, China needs to at least consider the influences of the exchange rate reform on many aspects, including macroeconomic stability, economic growth, employment, the financial system, the level of financial supervision, the tolerance of enterprises, foreign trade, relationship with neighboring countries and regions, the world economy, and international finance. During the reform, the Chinese government was always clear about the reasons, objectives, and steps of the reform, even though there were pressures from the outside world for each reform. Overall, the reform clearly shows that China, as a responsible country, has taken into consideration the influences of its reform on the economy and finance of surrounding countries and regions and even the world and that China has also followed market economy rules. When the timing is right, China will take the initiative to promote the reform even without external pressures. However, if the timing is not right, China won't rush into a reform, even under heavy external pressures.

Three Basic Principles in the Reform of the RMB Exchange Rate Setting Mechanism

During its reform, the Chinese government adhered to three basic principles, that is, independence, controllability, and progressiveness:

- Independence means that the government determines the methods, content, and timing of the reform according to the reform and development needs.
- Controllability means that various changes from the RMB exchange rate reform are controllable from the macroeconomic perspective. While proceeding with the reform, China maintains control of the macroeconomy to avoid financial market turmoil and wild economic fluctuations.
- Progressiveness means that China carries out the reform step by step according to market changes, taking stakeholders' tolerance into consideration.

Directions

The reform of the RMB exchange rate setting mechanism has promoted the development of China's foreign exchange market. However, the new system still needs to be improved and faces a series of problems: (1) expectations on RMB appreciation, (2) international trade conflicts, (3) the imbalance of the domestic industrial structure, and (4) abnormal growth of foreign exchange reserves. As the foreign exchange rate reform is facing severe challenges, China must pay great attention to the policy orientation of the RMB exchange rate while further proceeding with the reform.

First, it must clearly know the stage and background of the reform. At present, the foreign exchange market and its management system cannot fully satisfy the requirements of opening up to the outside world. As a developing country opening its door, China must insist that monetary policies will be independent and the opening of the capital account will be progressive. During this period, a flexible and managed floating exchange rate system is the natural result of the reform. This means that the exchange rate reform in the future will continue to be based on the framework of the managed floating rate system. There are mainly three directions to manage the fluctuation of the RMB exchange rate: (1) prevent excessive exchange rate fluctuations and speculation in the financial market from the macroeconomic perspective, (2) adjust the exchange rate in order to optimize resource allocation and achieve balance of international payments, and (3) accommodate the tolerance of most enterprises during the optimization of resource allocation and prevent large-scale bankruptcies and layoffs.

Second, China must insist on the priority of the exchange rate system. The reform of the system includes two aspects, the "mechanism" and the "level." It is not simply the level, nor the appreciation of RMB. The mechanism is the core of the system. Therefore, improving the exchange rate setting mechanism is the primary task of the RMB exchange rate system reform. Without a sound and complete mechanism, it will be impossible to keep the RMB exchange rate at a proper and balanced level. To perfect the exchange rate mechanism requires China to consider social and economic tolerance to prevent wild exchange rate fluctuations from happening. In this sense, the completion of the exchange rate mechanism reflects the principles of independence and progressiveness of the RMB exchange rate reform. Currently, the primary task is to actively implement RMB exchange rate policies, provided that exchange rates are stable. These policies include broadening the RMB fluctuating range, increasing the flexibility of RMB, improving the operating mechanism of foreign exchange rates, and expediting financial innovations for the foreign exchange market. In addition, the reform is a dynamic process. China should continue to improve the RMB exchange rate setting mechanism according to domestic situations and the principles of independence, progressiveness, and controllability so as to allow the market to play more roles in setting exchange rates and to promote market-oriented policies.

Feasible Ways to Increase the Flexibility of the RMB Exchange

There are three policy choices for the appreciation of RMB. The first is to keep RMB stable. The second is to announce a large surprise appreciation. The third is to effect slow, progressive appreciation by gradually increasing exchange rate flexibility. The first choice is difficult and costly to manage, the second is effective but destructive, and the third is relatively reasonable. Increasing the flexibility of RMB and progressive appreciation indicates that the appreciation range should be controlled according to the tolerance of the economy. Therefore, the central bank must balance inflation, currency appreciation, economic growth, and increasing employment. Progressive appreciation is beneficial not only to releasing the pressure of inflation and economic restructuring but also to long-term sustainable economic stability and growth in China and the world.

Third, China must maintain the progressive transition of the exchange rate system. A floating rate system needs support from a developed financial market. However, the Chinese financial market is still in its infancy. The foreign exchange market and financial entities are not fully developed, and their knowledge on risks and risk-hedging ability are rather low. Before the full development of the financial market and its entities, transforming the exchange rate system to the floating rate system will likely bring significant financial risks. Furthermore, as Chinese economic reform is progressive, the RMB exchange rate reform should also follow suit. In fact, in order to support progressive reform, the government has been making preparations for related economic policies such as easing market entry requirements, loosening restrictions on the purchase of foreign exchange by citizens and some enterprises, introducing forward RMB contracts and providing risk hedging tools to allow market participants to cope with the flexible rate mechanism, making further progress in reforming the banking system, and enhancing the financial system's risk-hedging capacities.

Fourth, China must continue to complete the monitoring mechanism for the RMB exchange rate. While promoting the market-oriented RMB exchange rate setting mechanism, it must establish and complete the monitoring mechanism, as is required by the needs of macroeconomic control and risk prevention, which also provide the government with an objective ground to propose exchange rate policies and make necessary adjustments. The monitoring mechanism includes both micro and macro mechanisms. From the micro monitoring perspective, by observing the changes of market entities Chinese authorities can learn entities' expectations on exchange rates, predict the trend of foreign exchange supply and demand, and accordingly determine whether the level of exchange rates is reasonable. From the macro perspective, by setting up the macro monitoring system they are able to know how the level of exchange rates changes macroeconomic indicators during a certain period and predict foreign exchange supply and demand as well as the market trend in the coming period, which serves as an objective basis for the exchange rate policy adjustment.

In summary, the RMB exchange rate system reform is a necessary process during financial reform and economic development. During the reform, China must adhere to the principle of progressiveness and make corresponding macroeconomic policies according to the changing economic environment. While improving the exchange rate system, it must also consider economic entities' tolerance and apply necessary supporting measures to ensure stable and sustainable long-term economic growth. Meanwhile, it must take advantage of the optimal timing to adjust the exchange rate system, accelerate adjustments to the economic structure and changes to the economic growth pattern, and fundamentally realize the stability and equilibrium of the RMB exchange rate.

CHAPTER 5

CAPITAL ACCOUNT OPENING IN CHINA

Capital account opening is China's inevitable choice during the integration of the economy and the currency into the world.

Current Chinese policy on the capital account may appear tight but is relatively loose in reality.

Opening the capital account in a gradual, orderly, and controllable manner is the basic Chinese model.

Opening the capital account is an intrinsic need of an open country during economic development. The history of the world economy shows that almost every country, whether a traditional economic powerhouse such as the United States or Great Britain or an emerging economy such as the BRICs (Brazil, Russia, India, and China), has been confronted with the problem of how to open the capital account during different periods of time. This issue is even more vital to China, as it is in an important period of economic and financial reforms.

Capital Account Opening Defined

The capital account belongs to the statistical category of the balance of international payments. Before 1993 the *Balance of Payments Manual* published by the IMF classified the statements of the balance of international payments into the current account and the capital account. The capital account is mainly responsible for the statistics of fund transfers between countries, including direct investment, portfolio investment, and other investment. The 1993 edition of the *Balance of Payments Manual* (fifth edition) classifies the capital account into the capital and financial account (Figure 5.1). However, in most research papers, people usually use the capital account to substitute the capital and financial account.

The Capital and Financial Account

The capital account consists of capital transfers and the acquisition or disposal of nonproduced, nonfinancial assets. Capital transfers are classified into three components: (1) the transfer of fixed asset ownership, (2) fund transfers related to or subjected to the acquisition or disposal of a fixed asset, and (3) the relief or dismissal of the debtor's financial liability without any repayment to the creditor by mutual agreement between the creditor and debtor. Acquisition or disposal of nonproduced, nonfinancial assets largely covers intangible assets, such as patented entities, leases or other transferable contracts, and goodwill.

Figure 5.1 The Capital Account and the Balance of International Payments

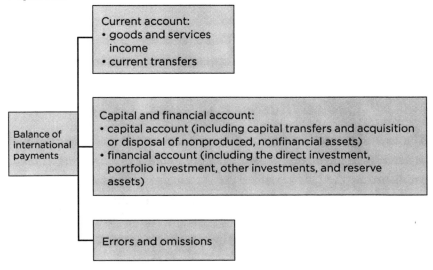

The financial account consists of ownership transactions by an entity to change its assets and liabilities. These transitions include direct investment, portfolio investment, other investment, and reserve assets. Direct investment reflects the lasting interest of a resident entity in one economy (investors) in a resident entity of another economy (direct investment enterprises), including all transactions between direct investors and direct investment enterprises. Portfolio investment includes transactions of equity securities and debt securities; the latter can be further classified into notes and bonds, money market instruments, and financial derivatives. Other investment includes short-term and long-term trade credit, loans, currency, and deposits as well as other payables or receivables. Reserve assets include transactions in assets that are considered by the monetary authority of one economy to be available for use in funding payment imbalances and, in some instances, meeting other financial needs.

The Trend of Capital Account
Opening Is Irreversible

Capital account opening refers to the dynamic process by which the capital account management system is transformed from under control to free from control.

Capital account opening technically has both a broad and narrow meaning. The narrow meaning of capital account opening is that no limitations are placed on cross-border capital transactions recorded in the capital and financial account category in the balance of international payments. In such a case, convertible currencies can flow in or out of a country without limitations. However, the transaction cannot be completed if transaction counterparties do not have a convertible currency and the country in which the transaction is executed forbids the exchange of the currency under the particular transaction. The broad meaning of capital account opening, however, eliminates such transaction limitations on cross-border capital flows. It also loosens foreign exchange control related to capital transactions, such as cross-border fund transfers, exchange of currencies, and so on.

Under the influence of economic integration and with increasing free trade and financial globalization, capital account opening has become an irreversible trend. Since the 1970s, developing countries have begun their financial reforms following developed countries. Primary measures included reforms of the inflexible financial system, reduction of interventions by the government in the financial market, easing of restrictions on financial institutions and the financial market, and promotion of market-oriented interest rates and exchange rates. The process of financial globalization is highlighted by globalization of the banking business, innovation of financial tools, liberalization of financial regulations, and eventual integration of the financial market. Capital account opening not only supports these four steps in the process of financial globalization but also becomes a necessary condition for financial globalization.

Capital Account Opening Advantages and Disadvantages

Generally speaking, capital account opening allows capital to flow freely across borders, effectively allocating resources in the world and raising overall economic efficiencies and social benefits. From the macroeconomic perspective, capital account opening can attract foreign capital and alleviate the problem of dual shortages that most developing countries face, that is, the shortage of savings and foreign exchange, hence encouraging investment and promoting economic growth. From the microeconomic perspective, capital account opening contributes to attracting foreign investments and introducing a competition mechanism, thus increasing domestic financial efficiency. Meanwhile, it also helps investors to freely allocate assets in the world to optimize their investment portfolios and reduce investment risks.

Of course, while capital account opening has these advantages, there are some potential uncertainties. Normally, after a nation opens up the capital account, international capital flows will increase, especially a large amount of short-term hot money flows, which will significantly increase financial market volatility and endanger the stability of the financial system. Actual situations in the past show that capital account opening since the 1970s caused more financial crisis, damaging the financial and industrial sectors in the country where the crisis occurred.

In summary, capital account opening has the following main risks: (1) According to the theory of the Impossible Trinity, international capital flows after the opening of the capital account will influence the effectiveness of the central bank's monetary policies. (2) After the opening of the capital account, a large amount of foreign capital will flow to a country that is expected to have favorable economic prospects and flow out of a country with worsening economic prospects, thus significantly increasing the fluctuations of each country's economic cycles. (3) Capital account opening is likely to increase competition among currencies, causing currency substitution and capital outflows, which will increase exchange rate volatility, discount the effectiveness of monetary policies, and damage the confidence of the public in domestic currency.

Currency Substitution

Currency substitution is a unique phenomenon of currency flows in an open economy. This phenomenon usually occurs when there are high expectations of the depreciation of the domestic currency. Under such a condition, the public decreases holdings of the less valuable domestic currency and increases holdings of the more valuable foreign currency, trying to lower opportunity costs and achieve relatively high returns, hence partially or completely replacing the domestic currency with a foreign currency. Contrary to Gresham's Law, currency substitution reflects the phenomenon of good money driving out the bad.

In summary, capital account opening has dual effects. The capital account provides international capital with more convenience and liquidity, which encourages and increases domestic investment, especially in countries that lack capital, bringing positive impacts on economic growth. On the other hand, capital account opening exposes a country's financial system to potential attacks by international hot money, which will likely increase economic fluctuations or financial system fragility, eventually increasing the likelihood of a financial crisis.

Comparisons of Capital Account Opening: Progressive versus Radical Approach

There are two capital account opening models, a progressive one and an aggressive one (see Figure 5.2). The former is a model to open up the capital account in an orderly and reasonable manner according to actual situations, whereas the latter insists on an "explosive" method.

In recent history, Latin American and Southeast Asian countries were frequently hit by financial crises, drawing people's attention to the unique situation in developing countries. Although some research pointed out that premature capital account opening in Latin American countries and Southeast Asian countries played an important role in triggering financial crises, the conclusion was quickly overturned and redirected to the premature and excessive financial freedom in some developing countries. This somewhat gave people an illusion that the relationship between capital account opening and financial crises was a unique phenomenon of financial freedom in most developing countries.

As a matter of fact, a financial crisis arising from capital account opening is not a phenomenon only in developing countries. Figure 5.3 clearly illustrates that countries such as France, Denmark, Italy, Finland, New Zealand, Portugal, Greece, and Mexico have all experienced similar financial crises during the period of rapidly opening up their capital account, which is shown by the charts with sharply rising curves. The result explains that capital account opening and financial

Figure 5.2 Comparison of Capital Account Opening Models

Aggressiveness (one step)   Progressiveness (step by step)

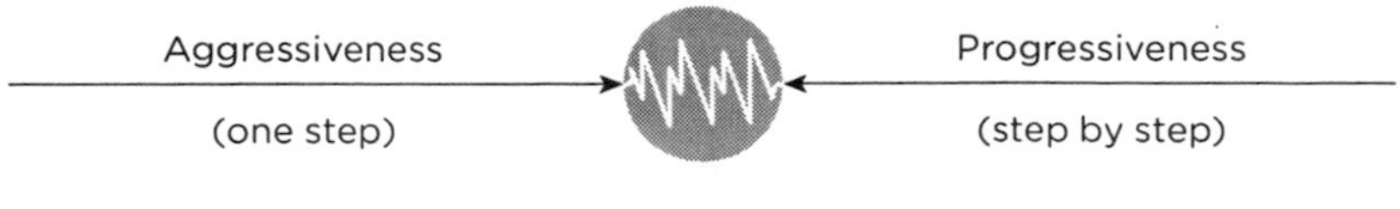

Figure 5.3 Capital Account Opening and Financial Crisis in Some Countries

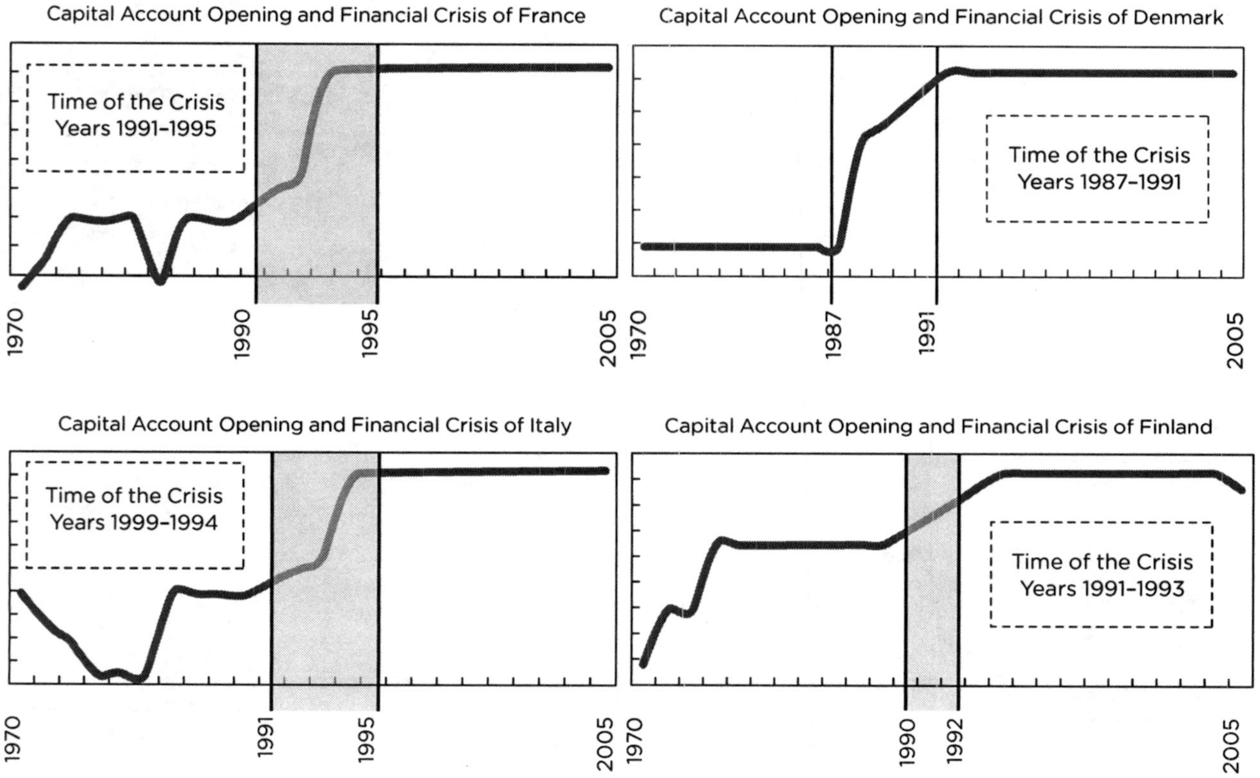

Capital Account Opening and Financial Crisis of Denmark

Time of the Crisis
Years 1987-1991

Capital Account Opening and Financial Crisis of Finland

Time of the Crisis
Years 1991-1993

Capital Account Opening and Financial Crisis of France

Time of the Crisis
Years 1991-1995

Capital Account Opening and Financial Crisis of Italy

Time of the Crisis
Years 1999-1994

(continued)

Figure 5.3 Capital Account Opening and Financial Crisis in Some Countries (continued)

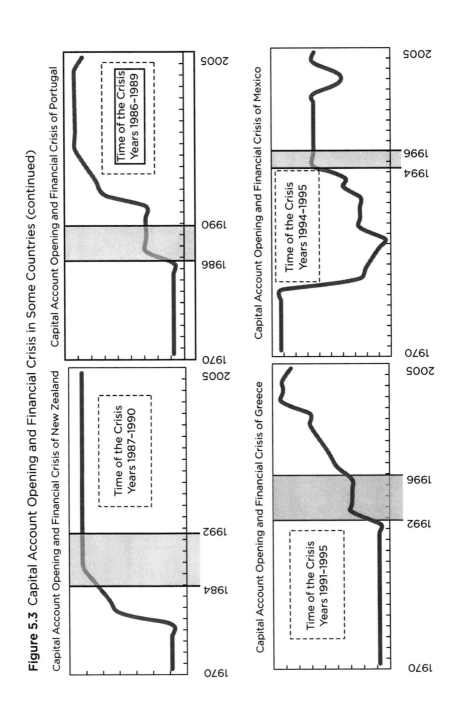

crises are not necessarily closely correlated with whether an economy is in a developing country or a developed country. They are likely to have a more common relationship.

Figure 5.3 graphically illustrates the close relationship between capital account opening and financial crises. As a matter of fact, according to statistics from *Global Development Finance* issued by the World Bank in 1998, many countries experienced a financial crisis within five years after capital account opening. Some countries even had repetitive financial crises (Table 5.1). Data provided by Hiro Ito and Menzie Chinn (2007) also demonstrates that the probability of having a financial crisis within five years after capital account opening can be as high as 60 percent.

The typical cases mentioned clearly show that whether in a developing country or a developed country, a financial crisis is usually accompanied by capital account opening. In a further analysis, Yulu Chen and Yong Ma (2010) studied 55 countries and demonstrated that from the perspective of inactive relationship between capital account opening and systemic financial crises, the opening model choice is more important than the degree of financial freedom, and that increasing the degree of long-term capital account opening will not trigger a financial crisis, but aggressive capital account opening will significantly increase the probability of a financial crisis.

The results of the above research reveal that capital account opening is a nation's choice of objectives for its long-term development strategy. Nevertheless, in terms of attaining the objectives, aggressive capital account opening should be avoided and progressive capital account opening is more conducive to financial stability.

China's Capital Account Opening: The Past and the Present

The opening of the Chinese capital account dated back to the middle of the 1990s. In 1994, the Chinese foreign exchange system underwent a significant reform. First, China used to have a policy that required selling foreign exchange to the state and retaining foreign exchange

Table 5.1 Capital Account Opening and Financial Crisis

Country (Year of Crisis)	Short-Term Capital Flows	Long-Term Capital Flows	A Crisis Occurred After Five Years?	Severity
Argentina (1980)	open	open	Y	Y
Argentina (1989)	close	close	NA	—
Argentina (1995)	open	open	Y	Y
Chile (1981)	open	open	Y	Y
Mexico (1994)	open	open	Y	Y
Venezuela (1994)	close	close	NA	—
Malaysia (1985)	open	open	Y	—
Philippines (1981)	close	close	N	—
Thailand (1997)	open	open	Y	Y
South Africa (1985)	close	open	Y	—
Turkey (1985)	open	close	Y	—
Turkey (1991)	open	open	Y	Y
America (1980)	open	open	N	—
Canada (1983)	open	open	N	—
Japan (1992)	open	open	N	—
France (1991)	open	open	Y	—
Italy (1990)	open	open	Y	—
Australia (1989)	open	open	Y	—
New Zealand (1989)	open	open	Y	—
Brazil (1994)	close	open	NA	—
Indonesia (1992)	open	open	N	—
South Korea (1985)	close	open	Y	—
Turkey (1994)	open	open	Y	—
Sri Lanka (1992)	close	open	Y	—

Source: World Bank, *Global Development Finance*, 1998.

quotas. After the reform, the mandatory plans and approval of using foreign currency were terminated. Second, the official RMB exchange rate was merged into the market rate to form a unified and managed floating exchange rate that was based on market demand and supply and allowed foreign currencies to trade within a certain range. Third, a unified, standardized, and efficient foreign exchange market was established. Fourth, pricing, settlement, and circulation of foreign currencies inside the country were prohibited. Foreign exchange certificates would no longer be issued. After the above-mentioned reforms, China successfully realized conditional convertibility of RMB for current account transactions in 1994.

Foreign Exchange Certificates

For travelers' convenience and to prevent the circulation and arbitrage of foreign currency and the illegal purchase of goods with foreign currency, the Bank of China on April 1, 1980, began to issue foreign exchange certificates denominated in RMB. Foreigners, overseas Chinese, compatriots from Hong Kong, Macao, and Taiwan, foreign embassies, and delegates were required to use foreign exchange certificates at hotels, restaurants, designated shops, and airports in exchange for goods and services. Any remaining certificates could be exchanged for the foreign currency at up to 50 percent of original value or carried abroad. Any entity accepting foreign exchange certificates had to receive prior approval from the Administration of Foreign Exchange, and foreign exchange certificates received had to be deposited in banks and managed separately based on their inflows and outflows. Any entity that received foreign exchange certificates might retain a portion of the foreign exchange accordingly if it sold certificates to a bank. Foreign exchange certificate issuance was stopped on January 1, 1994. Any certificates still in circulation remained effective until December 31, 1994. They could be exchanged for either U.S. dollars or RMB before June 30, 1995.

In the next three years, remaining exchange restrictions on current accounts were eliminated. On December 1, 1996, China formally accepted the obligations of Article VIII of the IMF's Articles of Agreement, removing exchange restrictions on current account transactions. Therefore, RMB has been fully convertible under the current account since then.

Since 1996 China has moved forward with the reform of foreign exchange management and gradually opened up capital account transactions according to economic development. The goal for managing foreign exchange under the capital account was changed to maintain the independence of the monetary policy, stabilize the nominal RMB exchange rate, maintain the balance of international payments, and prevent financial crises.

As China joined the WTO in 2001, capital account opening was further broadened to keep the promise of financial opening. Especially since 2002, as China faced more pressures from currency appreciation and excessive accumulation of foreign currency reserves, capital account opening has been accelerated. Several major events occurred, including loosening restrictions on foreign investment by domestic enterprises, introducing the Qualified Foreign Institutional Investors (QFII), permitting international financial institutions to issue yuan-denominated bonds in China, allowing insurance companies and insurance asset management companies to invest in overseas markets using their own foreign exchange, introducing the Qualified Domestic Institutional Investors (QDII), allowing foreign residents with Chinese citizenship to transfer domestic assets outside China, allowing foreign residents who inherit domestic assets to transfer the assets outside China, increasing the RMB limit for Chinese citizens and foreigners to carry when crossing the border, and increasing the limit of foreign exchange that an individual is allowed to purchase annually. Table 5.2 has the details.

The QFII and QDII System

The QFII (Qualified Foreign Institutional Investors) system refers to a kind of market opening model under which qualified foreign

Table 5.2 The Process of China's Capital Account Opening

Main Content	Major Events
Loosening restrictions on foreign investment by domestic enterprises	• A pilot program was executed to reform investing in foreign countries by several provinces and cities beginning in October 2002. • In May 2005 the SAFE issued a notice regarding certain issues associated with expanding the test reform on the control of foreign exchange for investment in foreign countries and extended the test reform to all regions in China. • The quota of foreign exchange that China could use to invest in foreign countries was increased from US$3.3 billion to US$5 billion in 2005. The approval authority of each SAFE regional agency on sources of foreign exchange for overseas investment was also increased from US$3 million to US$10 million.
Introducing the Qualified Foreign Institutional Investors (QFII)	• In December 2002 the SAFE and the China Security Regulatory Commission jointly announced the start of QFII. • Any QFII that received approval from the China Security Regulatory Commission and the SAFE was allowed to invest in the Chinese securities market, including equities, bonds, mutual funds, and other financial instruments denominated in the Chinese yuan. • Ninety-nine foreign financial institutions have been qualified as QFII.
Permitting international financial institutions to issue yuan-denominated bonds in China	• At the end of 2004 the Ministry of Finance approved three foreign financial institutions to issue bonds in China denominated in the Chinese yuan that were worth 4 billion. • In March 2005 the People's Bank of China and three other ministries or commissions jointly announced Temporary Measures on Yuan-Denominated Bonds Issued by International Development Agencies, limiting bond issuers to international development agencies and requiring issuers to have at least an AA credit rating for yuan-denominated bonds and have existing loans to or investments over US$1 billion in any domestic Chinese project or enterprise.

(continued)

Table 5.2 The Process of China's Capital Account Opening (continued)

Main Content	Major Events
Allowing insurance companies and insurance asset management companies to invest in overseas markets using their own foreign exchange	• In August 2004 the China Insurance Regulatory Commission and the People's Bank of China jointly announced Temporary Measures on the Use of Foreign Exchange Insurance Proceeds in Foreign Countries, allowing insurance companies and insurance asset managing companies to invest in overseas markets using their own foreign exchange to expand the investment channels for insurance proceeds and more sufficiently diversify investment risks.
Introducing the Qualified Domestic Institutional Investors (QDII)	• In April 2006 the People's Bank of China, the China Banking Regulatory Commission, and the SAFE jointly announced Temporary Measures on the Management of Clients' Overseas Assets by Commercial Banks, embarking on the execution of QDII. • In August 2006 the China Banking Regulatory Commission approved 11 domestic commercial banks and 8 foreign banks to develop products for QDII. • In September 2006 the SAFE approved US$500 million investments by HuaAn Funds in overseas markets and announced the Notice on Certain Issues Associated with Foreign Exchange for Overseas Investment in Securities by Fund Management Companies. China Life Insurance Co., Tai Kang Life Insurance Co., and other insurance companies obtained qualifications as QDII.
Other measures associated with foreign investment	• In November 2004 the People's Bank of China announced Temporary Measures on the Management of Foreign Exchange Associated with Individual Asset Transfers, which allowed foreign residents with Chinese citizenship to transfer domestic assets outside China and allowed foreign residents who inherited domestic assets to transfer the assets outside China. • From January 1, 2005, the RMB limit that Chinese citizens and foreigners were allowed to carry when crossing the border was increased from 6,000 yuan to 20,000 yuan. • From February 1, 2007, the limit on foreign exchange that an individual was allowed to purchase annually was increased from US$20,000 to US$50,000.

institutional investors can transfer a certain amount of foreign exchange into China in accordance with related regulations and limits, convert it into RMB, invest in the Chinese securities market using the strictly supervised special investment account, and transfer any capital gain or interest income outside China with prior approval. As of September 1, 2009, when Fidelity Mutual Fund Co. (Hong Kong) received the QFII qualification, there were a total of 99 QFII members approved by the China Securities Regulatory Commission. Similar to the QFII, the QDII (Qualified Domestic Institutional Investors) system is an investment system under which any domestic financial investment institution accredited by the government is allowed to invest in the foreign financial markets before the capital account is completely open. By August 2010 there were a total of 23 QDII funds either in operation or being launched in China. (See Figure 5.4 for QFII and QDII approved investment amounts.)

Figure 5.4 Total Approved QFII and QDII Investment Amounts

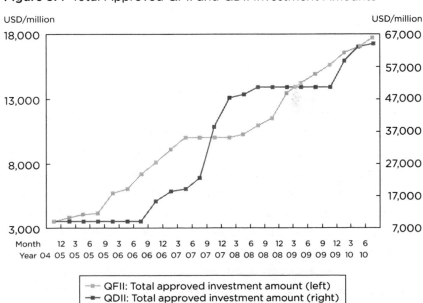

USD/million

USD/million

QFII: Total approved investment amount (left)
QDII: Total approved investment amount (right)

Source: State Administration of Foreign Exchange.

Current Capital Account Opening in China
"Appears Tight but Loose in Reality"

From 1996 the IMF used the capital transaction categories from the Organisation for Economic Co-operation and Development (OECD) and classified the capital account accordingly in the *Annual Report on Exchange Arrangements and Exchange Restrictions* (AREAER). The capital account transactions can be divided into 13 categories according to the appendix of the AREAER.

Even in developed countries that have fully opened the capital account, there are some regulations on certain subitems of the capital account. Taking 2003 statistical data (Table 5.3) as an example, we can see there are 4, 2, 4, 1, and 3 subitems of the total 13 capital account categories that are under control by the United States, Great Britain, France, Germany, and Japan respectively.

Capital account opening is not an absolute concept. Ideal capital account opening does not mean totally or absolutely opening up. Since the 1980s, developed countries have largely opened up their capital account. But they adopted policies that appeared loose but were tight in reality, with the purpose of protecting the domestic economy and financial system. On the contrary, China is now adopting an opening model that appears tight but is loose in reality; that is, controls on the capital account are quite loose even though there seem to be strict regulations on some subitems of the capital account, either in name or in theory (Table 5.4). As early as 2001, within the total of 43 capital account transactions China completely opened 12 items, partially opened 16 items, and prohibited only 15 items.

According to statistical data from the IMF, of 43 capital account items, about 50 percent currently have no or little control in China; only 10 percent are strictly controlled, most of which are associated with nonresidents selling or issuing money market instruments and derivatives inside China and residents and nonresidents providing personal loans.

In recent years, scholars from China and abroad conducted empirical research on China's capital account opening and reached

Table 5.3 An Outline of IMF Members' Current and Capital Account Transactions Monitoring Framework

Transactions of the Capital Account	Number of Countries	U.S.A.	Great Britain	France	Germany	Japan
Regulations and controls on securities transactions	133	*				
Regulations and controls on money market tools	115	*		*		
Regulations and controls on portfolio investment	103	*		*		
Regulations and controls on derivatives and other transactional tools	87					
Commercial credit	105					
Financial credit	112					
Guaranty, insurance, and standby financing instruments	88					
Regulations and controls on direct investment	149	*	*	*		*
Regulations and controls on direct investment liquidations	52					
Regulations and controls on real estate transactions	134					
Regulations and controls on personal fund flows	82					
Clauses applied specifically to commercial banks and other lending institutions	155		*			*

Source: Wang Guogang (2003).

Table 5.4 An Incomplete List of Capital Account Opening Items in China

Items	Specific Regulations
Capital and money market instruments	
1. Securities transactions in capital markets	
A. Purchase and sale of stocks or other equity securities	
Purchase by nonresidents inside the country	QFII with approved quotas can purchase A shares in the domestic stock market; nonresidents can purchase B shares.
Sale or issuance by nonresidents inside the country	Nonresidents can sell A shares or B shares, but do not have the right to issue these shares.
Purchase by residents in foreign markets	With approved quotas, QDII can invest in foreign stocks.
Sale or issuance by residents in foreign markets	Nonresidents can sell A shares or B shares but do not have the right to issue these shares.
B. Bonds and other debt securities	
Purchase by nonresidents inside the country	QFII can purchase corporate bonds, convertible bonds, and government bonds.
Sale or issuance by nonresidents inside the country	International development agencies with an authorization from the Ministry of Commerce or the People's Bank of China or the National Development and Reform Commission can issue RMB-denominated securities.
Purchase by residents in foreign markets	Qualified domestic commercial banks, mutual fund companies, and insurance companies can invest in overseas bonds. Domestic commercial banks can invest residents' RMB or foreign exchange directly in overseas fixed income products.
Sale or issuance by residents in foreign markets	Residents can issue foreign bonds with the permission of the National Development and Reform Commission, the State Administration of Foreign Exchange, and the State Council.

2. Money market instruments

Purchase by nonresidents inside the country

QFII can invest in money market funds.

Sale or issuance by nonresidents inside the country

Forbidden.

Purchase by residents in foreign markets

The regulations on the purchase of bonds or other debt securities in foreign markets are applicable.

Sale or issuance by residents in foreign markets

With the permission of the State Administration of Foreign Exchange, residents can issue short-term (less than a year) securities, such as commercial paper.

3. Collective investment securities

Purchase by nonresidents inside the country

QFII can invest in closed-end or open-end mutual funds.

Sale or issuance by nonresidents inside the country

Forbidden.

Purchase by residents in foreign markets

The regulations on the purchase of bonds or other debt securities overseas are applicable.

Sale or issuance by residents in foreign markets

The regulations on sale or issuance of money market instruments overseas are applicable.

Regulations on derivatives and other financial instruments

Purchase by nonresidents inside the country

Forbidden.

Sale or issuance by nonresidents inside the country

Forbidden.

Purchase by residents in foreign markets

Before purchasing, selling, or issuing financial derivatives in overseas markets, the qualifications of the domestic financial institution will be examined and foreign exchange exposures will be monitored.

Table 5.4 An Incomplete List of Capital Account Opening Items in China (continued)

Items	Specific Regulations
Sale or issuance by residents in foreign markets	
Regulations on credit operations	
1. Commercial credit	
From residents to nonresidents	Basically free from restrictions. Commercial credit from domestic financial institutions should receive approval from the State Administration of Foreign Exchange.
From nonresidents to residents	Restricted by related provisions in the Announcement on the Issues Associated with Perfecting Foreign Debt Management.
2. Financial credit	
From residents to nonresidents	The applicable rules are the same as those on commercial credit.
From nonresidents to residents	The applicable rules are the same as those on commercial credit.
3. Guaranty, insurance, and standby financing instruments	
From residents to nonresidents	Registration is required and some business need prior approval.
From nonresidents to residents	Companies with foreign ownership may be guaranteed by foreign institutions.
Regulations on direct investments	
1. Direct investments in foreign countries	
A. Expanding or establishing a new company or a subsidiary, or making an acquisition	The quota on foreign exchange for the purpose of foreign direct investments has been lifted. There are few regulations currently.

B. Buying into a newly established company or existing company	
2. Direct investments in China	Related laws and regulations must be obeyed. There are almost no restrictions.
A. Expanding or establishing a new company or a subsidiary, or making an acquisition	
B. Buying into a newly established company or existing company	
Regulations on direct investment liquidation	No restrictions.
Regulations on real estate transactions	
Purchase by residents in foreign countries	No restrictions.
Purchase by nonresidents inside China	Any foreign currency over US$50,000 to be converted to RMB must have permission from the State Administration of Foreign Exchange. Beginning in July 2006, any qualified nonresident can purchase a property only as a primary residence and for his or her own use in China.
Selling by nonresidents inside China	Proceeds from the sale of personal property can be transferred to foreign exchange and wired overseas only with prior permission from the State Administration of Foreign Exchange.
Regulations on personal funds flows	
1. Loans	
From residents to nonresidents	Under supervision and controls.
From nonresidents to residents	Under supervision and controls.

Table 5.4 An Incomplete List of Capital Account Opening Items in China (continued)

Items	Specific Regulations
2. Gifts, donations, and inheritance	Any gift or donation under US$50,000 from a Chinese resident to any nonresident is allowed by verifying his or her personal ID. If the value exceeds US$50,000, the transaction shall provide properly notarized documentation. There is no restriction on the transfer of inheritance.
From nonresidents to residents	Certain documentation is needed, such as personal ID and the certificate of property ownership.
3. Settlement of debt by an immigrant in a foreign country	
4. Transfer of assets	
Immigrants transferring assets abroad	The transferor should send one application to the State Administration of Foreign Exchange to transfer all personal assets. If the amount exceeds RMB200,000, the amount over RMB200,000 needs to be transferred step by step.
Immigrants transferring assets to China	
5. Transfer of award or lottery money	

Source: Research Report on Chinese Capital Market (2010).

a consistent result, suggesting that its capital account opening is at a medium level compared to the other countries in the same period.

China's Capital Account Opening Model: Objectives and Orders

Whether a country can smoothly achieve capital account opening without affecting its economic and financial stability is closely related to its domestic and international economic and financial environment. The basic requirements for a country to open its capital account include a stable political and economic environment both at home and abroad, effective macroeconomic control and financial supervision capacity, competitive enterprises, a financial market with sufficient depth and breadth, a sound legal system, and a transparent information disclosure mechanism.

As a typical developing country, China still hasn't had the prerequisite for the complete opening of the capital account. If China adopts the aggressive model to abruptly open the capital account once and for all, it may encounter various uncertainties and risks. Therefore, it is crucial for China to fully balance the risks and benefits of opening the capital account to ensure macroeconomic and financial stability. Jagdis Bhagwati (1998) once said: "Any country that intends to realize the free flow of capital must weigh the pros and cons as well as consider the possibility of a crisis. Even if as some people assume that the free flow of capital will not lead to a crisis, a wise decision can not be made unless gains from improved economic efficiency are weighed against all potential losses."

Based on capital account opening situations in other countries and the current situations in China, the progressive opening model should be the best choice for China. Using this model, China will follow the principle of opening the capital account in a gradual, orderly, and controllable manner. The progressive model will allow China to gradually open up the capital account while maximally ensuring macroeconomic and financial stability and avoiding various potential risks inherent in the aggressive model.

China's Capital Account Opening Timetable

Although China does not give an accurate timetable for the capital account opening, the gradual opening of the capital account in China is the overall trend. As capital account opening is a complex, systematic project and is closely related to a country's economic development as well as its domestic and international political and economic environment, it is not realistic to come up with a precise timetable. However, by learning from the experience of developed countries, China can roughly estimate the timing to achieve the complete opening of the capital account.

The process by which major world economies introduced convertible currencies shows that it took Japan, Great Britain, and Germany 16, 18, and 20 years respectively to open their capital accounts after opening their current accounts. The gradual opening of the capital account generally requires 15 to 20 years. Given that Chinese economic and financial development still lags behind the above-mentioned three countries, China will need more time to complete capital account opening after current account opening than the average of these three countries. Benchmarking against Germany, which used the longest time among these three countries, we can estimate that after China realized current account convertibility in 1996, the convertibility of RMB for capital account transactions should be completed between 2015 and 2020 (Figure 5.5). The time interval happens to be consistent with the period of a strategic opportunity in the process of Chinese economic development.

Figure 5.5 Time from Current Account Opening to Capital Account Opening for Some World Nations

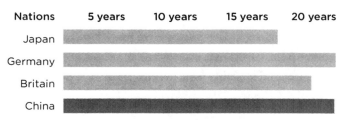

The Order and Principle of China's Capital Account Opening

As China gradually opens up the capital account, it will inevitably be confronted with issues of how to define and manage the pace and order of opening the capital account as well as its subitems. After long-term analysis and research, Chinese scholars have reached a conclusion on the best order, based on China's actual conditions and the experience of other countries. The best order should be as follows: capital inflows first and capital outflows next; direct investment first and portfolio investment next; portfolio investment first and bank credit next; long-term investment first and short-term investment next; institutions first and individuals next; debt securities first and equities and derivatives next; offering markets first and trading markets next; transactions backed by a true deal first and transactions not backed by a true deal next. The execution of opening the capital account demonstrates that China has been basically following this plan.

In the meantime, China's capital account opening should also observe the following three basic principles.

Risk control principle

During the opening of the capital account, a country normally opens an account item with a lower risk first, followed by an account item with a higher risk, which is the most important principle of other countries in determining the capital account opening order. For example, it is believed that long-term capital transactions should be opened before short-term capital transactions, transactions backed by a true deal should be opened before transactions not backed by a true deal, and institutional transactions should be opened before individual transactions, all of which reflect the risk control principle.

Goal-oriented principle

A country's selection of the capital account opening order should be compatible with its strategic objectives, because capital account opening has always been focused on economic development. For instance, developing countries prefer to open foreign direct investment first due to lack of capital, technology, and managerial skills. However, developed countries with excess capital prefer to encourage their domestic companies to invest overseas and lift the associated controls on capital at an early stage.

Conditional restriction principle

Capital account opening depends heavily on domestic and international economic and financial conditions. Therefore, the capital account opening order and pattern are consistent with conditions. For example, a country with an immature domestic financial market should be very cautious when adopting the policies of opening the capital account.

Capital account opening is not a separate issue related to foreign exchange control but a system project interrelated with the reform of the domestic economy and financial system. Capital account opening should proceed in coordination with interest rate reform, exchange rate reform, and reform on managing exchange reserves. Only in this way can China realize the capital account opening without affecting economic stability and contribute to the recovery and stability of the Chinese and world economies during the postcrisis period. As a matter of fact, the Chinese Twelfth Five-Year Plan clearly pointed out the need for "steadily proceeding with the market-oriented interest rate reform, improving the managed floating exchange rate system to be based on demand and supply, reforming the management of foreign exchange reserves, and gradually accomplishing the convertibility of RMB for capital account transactions."

CHAPTER 6

INTERNATIONAL MONETARY SYSTEM REFORM AND RMB GLOBALIZATION

From the British pound to the U.S. dollar—is the Chinese yuan the next?

Competition between major economies and their currencies will eventually determine the direction of international currency reforms in the postcrisis era.

With China's economic development and full financial opening, the globalization of RMB is the trend.

The changes of global currencies and their exchange rates, together with the rise and fall of the global economy, highlight international monetary system transformations of the past 200 years. The changes of global currencies describe the transition of the international economic power and changes in the world economic pattern, while the changes of exchange rates reflect the incompatibility of interests in financial competition among many countries, especially large countries, and the need for a stable world monetary order. Since the nineteenth century, the evolution of five generations of the international monetary system has shown that increasing globalization requires a stable and balanced international monetary network. The international monetary system should correspond to the economic power of large monetary countries in order to maintain continuous stability.

The transition of the world currency system indicates that a nation's currency cannot become a part of the international reserve without having both strong economic power and comprehensive national strength. In essence, strong economic power is the economic foundation as well as the effective guarantee for the globalization of its currency. Currency globalization is a representation of a nation's economic and comprehensive power. Only after a nation strengthens its economic power and comprehensive national strength can it increase its share of output and trade in the world economy and expand its currency circulation and trade areas, bringing more demand for its currency. Besides, strong economic power is the basis for establishing credibility and reputation in the international community. Therefore, a nation must have economic support for its currency to be international. Actually, based on the study by Mundell (1999), strong currencies have always been closely related to strong economic power in the history of currency evolution (Table 6.1). Changing international reserve currencies in modern history demonstrate that strong economic power is the foundation and reason for either the replacement of the British pound by the U.S. dollar or the rise of the euro as an important international reserve currency.

It is necessary to point out that after Richard Nixon announced the termination of the dollar-to-gold link (terminating exchange of the U.S. dollar for gold) in 1971 and major currencies gradually changed to the floating exchange rate, efforts to reform and reconstruct a world currency system have never ended. Latin America's debt crisis in the 1980s, the Asian financial crisis in the 1990s, and the global financial crisis stemming from the American subprime mortgage crisis in 2007 demonstrate that the calls for reforms have been increasingly urgent.

As economic globalization continues around the world, reform of the international monetary system also faces transitioning from a unilateral structure to a multilateral structure. This means that—aside from the U.S. dollar,—the euro, the British pound, the Chinese yuan, and the Japanese yen will need to play more important roles in international settlement so as to establish a multilateral international monetary system that consists of the currencies of major world economies.

Throughout the history of the international monetary system, it is not difficult to find that the reconstruction of the international

Table 6.1 The Development of Strong Currencies: Strong Currencies and Strong Economies

Country (Sovereign Power)	Period	Gold Coin	Silver Coin	Currency
Greece	7th–3rd century BC	stater	tetradrachma	
Persia	6th–4th century BC	darics	shekels	
Macedonia	4th–2nd century BC	stater		
Rome	2nd century BC–4th century	aureus	denarius	
Byzantine	5th–13th century	solidus	stavraton	
Islam	7th–14th century	dinar	dirham	
Franks	8th–11th century		denier	
Italian City-states	13th–18th century	ducat, florin		
France	13th–18th century	deniers	livre	
The Netherlands	17th–18th century	guilder	stuiver	stuiver
Germany	14th–19th century		thaler	
France	1803–1870	20/40 franc	franc	
Great Britain	1820–1914	pound sterling	shilling	pound note
United States	1915 till now	eagle coin	dollar	dollar greenback
European Union				euro

Source: Robert A. Mundell (1999).

monetary system is fundamentally dependent upon the changes of world major economies. Because the costs associated with the changes are very high, and changes of the international monetary system structure usually lag behind changes of world economic powers, the transition will be a progressive, incremental, and long-term process. The replacement of the British pound by the U.S. dollar took almost a century and happened approximately 50 years after the United States overtook Great Britain as the world's economic leader. In the meantime, major economies participated in world wars or implemented self-centered fiscal and monetary policies in the middle of the transitioning process, forcing peripheral countries to break away from their monetary system and eventually igniting the fire of a fundamental reform.

The International Monetary System

Generally speaking, the international monetary system, or IMS, is the generic term for monetary rules and institutions related to international payments and trade. More specifically, it includes each nation's currency and its exchange rate system, international monetary and financial intervention and coordination rules, as well as the institutions that support these rules. An ideal international monetary system should feature stable currencies, stable finance, balanced growth, and symmetrical adjustment.

International Monetary System Transformations: Four Stages and Three Currency Substitutions

The international monetary system can be divided into four stages involving three currency substitutions over the past 200 years.

Not only did Great Britain and the United States firmly control the global economy and trade but their currencies also enjoyed unshakable power all over the world, and the British pound substituted for gold as the global medium of exchange. After World War II, the U.S.

dollar replaced the British pound as the standard international currency. During the next 60 years, the German deutsche mark, the Japanese yen, and the euro would come and go. The competition among currencies has been accompanied by changing economic and political power among major countries.

The first generation of the international monetary system came into being around the 1870s. It included the gold standard and the gold exchange standard. This system originated from the domination of Great Britain in the economic and trade areas and the final establishment of the gold standard in major developed countries. After winning in the 100 years of war that lasted from the seventeenth to the eighteenth century and stretched over Europe, Asia, and America, Britain became the first international economic hegemon following the successful Industrial Revolution. In 1819, by approving the Expediency of the Bank Resuming Cash Payments, Britain restored the fixed exchange rates between currency and gold and officially established the gold standard. After that, Germany, the United States, and France adopted the gold standard in 1871, 1873, and 1878 respectively, symbolizing the official establishment of the first-generation monetary system.

With the help of its advanced financial system and stable currency, Britain dominated the monetary system during this period. Both the British pound and gold served as the international standard currency. In 1914 direct exchange between gold and currency for each nation was suspended due to the World War I. Most countries adopted a floating exchange rate system to avoid the withdrawal of gold reserves. At the Genoa Conference in 1922, Britain, France, Italy, and Japan accepted the principle of restoring the gold standard. Because the gold supply at that time could not meet the demand for reserves by central banks all over the world, the gold exchange standard was initiated, that is, smaller countries used the currencies of major countries as their international reserves, and major countries used gold as international reserves.

In 1933 the dominance of the British pound abated, and the U.S. dollar and the French franc rose. As a result, the second-generation international monetary system developed. The British pound, the U.S. dollar, and the franc jointly acted as the international currency. During this period, these three monetary groups were equally powerful. They used their own currency as the main source of international reserves and method of payments. The parallel competition among these three currencies lasted until the end of World War II.

Two world wars and the economic crisis from 1929 to 1933 changed the status of the economic and political power between Great Britain and the United States. On one hand, the U.S. economy grew rapidly and overtook Britain as the leading power in the international financial market. On the other hand, the British economy suffered from significant damage due to the world war and was gradually declining. In July 1944, at an international monetary and financial conference held by allied countries at Bretton Woods in the United States, the White Plan defeated the Keynes Plan and became the basis of the International Monetary Fund Agreement. The third-generation monetary system was established, known as the Bretton Woods system, which confirmed the supreme status of the U.S. dollar in the international monetary system.

White Plan versus Keynes Plan

In 1940 Harry Dexter White, assistant to the U.S. secretary of the treasury, proposed a plan to manage future international finance known as the White Plan. The plan suggested establishing a stable international monetary fund with the total amount of at least US$5 billion, which would be contributed by member countries in gold, currencies, or government bonds. The quota would decide the voting right of each member country. This fund organization would issue Unita, a measurement of an international currency that could be freely exchanged for gold. Each member country's currency would have a fixed par value against Unita and remain unchanged except with prior permission. The plan also required that all member countries would have to establish fixed exchange rates that could be changed only with the permission of the organization at the time of an international payment imbalance.

The main mission of the fund was to maintain the international monetary order, especially stable exchange rates, and to solve the problem of imbalance in international payments.

In 1941 John Maynard Keynes, consultant for the British Treasury, proposed the Keynes Plan that called for the establishment of an international central bank and international clearing union, and the issuance of Bancor, an international payment unit based on gold. Bancor would be equal to gold and each country would mark its currency against Bancor. Each country would settle and clear its bonds and debts with its Bancor deposit account at the international clearing union and make adjustments to its international payments.

After World War II, the economies of Japan, Germany, and other main industrial countries grew very fast. America still had the strongest economic power, but its leading position was increasingly challenged, and the dollar-based international monetary system was getting more and more unstable. The Triffin Dilemma, deeply rooted in the third-generation international monetary system, couldn't be solved, and the working rules and basis of the international monetary system were gradually corroded. After several futile international rescue efforts in the first half of the 1970s, the Bretton Woods system finally collapsed. In 1976 the Jamaica Agreement was reached by an IMF committee. A new international monetary system known as the Jamaica system was formed. The Jamaica system is a milestone in the history of the international monetary system. Since then, human beings have completed the transition from commodity-based currencies to credit-based currencies, from a system with an anchor currency to one without an anchor currency, and from fixed exchange rates to floating exchange rates.

The Triffin Dilemma

The Triffin Dilemma or Triffin Paradox is a famous problem in the international monetary system. It was proposed by American economist

Robert Triffin after thorough research on the Bretton Woods system. In 1960, in his book *Gold and the Dollar Crisis: The Future of Convertibility*, he described the contradiction rooted in the Bretton Woods system. Since the U.S. dollar was linked to gold and other countries' currencies were linked to the U.S. dollar, the United States obtained the core status in the international monetary system. However, as other countries had to use U.S. dollars as payment in international trade and for reserve currency as well, the U.S. dollar would continue to accumulate offshore. This would mean a long-term trade deficit for the United States. On the contrary, the prerequisite of the U.S. dollar as the core international currency was based on the stability and strength of the U.S. dollar, requiring that the United States be a country with a long-term trade surplus. These two conditions would conflict with each other and thus constitute a paradox.

The fourth-generation international monetary system is also known as "multicurrencies with a dominant one." The dominant currency is the U.S. dollar, and multicurrencies refer to EUR, JPY, and GBP. In this system, the U.S. dollar still has the absolute advantage, although it is losing its monopoly. It is the most important reserve currency, means of payment and settlement, and unit of accounting in the world. Thus this system can also be called the dollar standard. According to IMF statistics, at the end of 2009 the U.S. dollar accounted for 64 percent of global official foreign reserves; 45 percent of global bonds were dominated and settled in USD; and 86 percent of global foreign exchange trade was against USD (where the total percentage was 200 percent, each trade concerning two currencies). There were 68 countries whose currencies were pegged or linked to the U.S. dollar. In this system, each country chooses its own exchange rate mechanism, which is pegged to either a single currency or a basket of currencies, and uses either a managed floating exchange rate system or a freely floating exchange rate system.

Overall, the international monetary system has undergone four primary stages and three currency substitutions during the last 200 years. There are three lessons from the international monetary system transformations during this process: (1) The structure of the international monetary system should be primarily consistent with key nations' economic power. (2) The breakout of a war with a key nation is an important condition for "igniting" the transformation of the international monetary system. (3) As the international monetary system transformation lags significantly behind the changes of key nations' economic power, the process will be long and gradual.

Current Status of the International Monetary System: Defects of the Dollar Standard

Theoretically speaking, a reasonable international monetary system should not only help maintain currency and financial stability but also promote global economic development. Although the current international monetary system has played an important role in solving the Triffin Dilemma to some extent, changing the inflexible exchange rate system, and promoting economic growth, it is still an unsystematic system, unable to be an ideal model for the international monetary system.

The First Limitation: Global Economic and Financial Imbalance

In the dollar standard system, developed countries led by the United States are considered to be the core countries, while emerging economies, such as China, and resource exporters, such as the Middle East countries, are considered peripheral countries (Figure 6.1). Consumer products and natural resources from peripheral countries flow into the United States in exchange for the U.S. dollars, enabling these countries to accumulate huge trade surpluses and foreign exchange reserves. Meanwhile, these countries invest a large amount of foreign exchange in U.S. securities, such as treasury notes and bonds, allowing the dollars to flow back to the United States. On the other hand, the United States cannot only import goods and natural resources at low prices but also enjoy the benefit of having the dollar flow back.

The "double circulation" of the physical resources and financial capital leads to the imbalance of international payments around the world. This is reflected in two aspects, the imbalance of international

Figure 6.1 Double Circulation of Physical Resources and Financial Capital Between Core Countries and Peripheral Countries

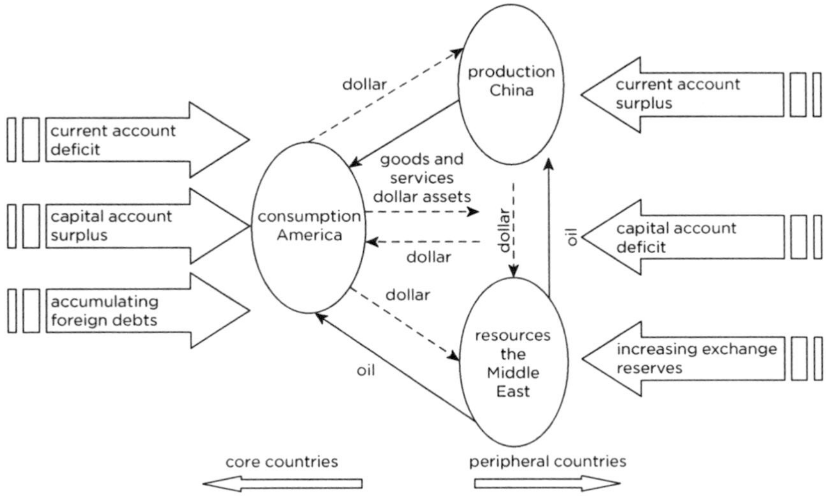

Note: Solid arrows stand for the flow of physical resources and dotted arrows stand for the flow of financial capital.
Source: Li Ruogu (2009).

trade and the imbalance of international capital flows. The former is due to large U.S. trade deficits with peripheral countries and the latter is due to continuous capital flows from the peripheral countries to the United States. According to statistics, about 86 percent of global capital flowed into developed economies such as the United States, Japan, Great Britain, and the Euro zone nations from 1999 to 2007.

In the past few years, the imbalance of international payments seems to have deteriorated. If either the sum of the absolute value of each nation's current account balance divided by the world total GDP, or the total world foreign currency reserves, is used as an estimate of the imbalance of international payments for the world, we can see that the former ratio rises from 3.7 percent in 2000 to 5.9 percent in 2008 and the latter amount rises from US$1.6 trillion in 1998 to US$8.1 trillion in 2008, about four times higher.

The basic model of global economic growth and balance has taken the following path since 2000. Emerging economies adopted a managed floating exchange rate system and used the middle rate to largely peg to the U.S. dollar to execute the development strategy led by exports to generate employment and growth, meanwhile attracting foreign direct investment to increase the efficiency of resource allocations and using U.S. dollar reserves to intervene in the foreign exchange market. On the other hand, countries that issue reserve currencies adopted an easy monetary policy to take advantage of low financing costs due to huge inflows of capital from emerging markets, as well as the wealth effect from asset bubbles, so as to generate economic growth and employment led by consumer consumption. As this model tends to cause asset bubbles to burst and trigger a financial crisis, it is considered a "horrible balance" of the world economy, referring to the paradox of economic growth and balance inherent in the model.

Generally speaking, peripheral countries are in a disadvantaged position in the international monetary system using the dollar standard. They absorb the majority of the cost. "The accumulation of foreign exchange by non-reserve countries means that the richest country in the world, the U.S., can get cheap capital, while poor countries are not only unable to access to cheap capital, but also have to bear reserve currencies' investment risks," Joseph Stiglitz once said. Moreover, there is also imbalance in terms of global coordination efforts under the existing international monetary system. The International Monetary Fund, the World Bank, and the World Trade Organization are three major international organizations created since World War II. However, a few developed countries maintain supermajority power in these organizations, while developing countries are at an obvious disadvantage and lack sufficient voting power, even though they significantly outnumber developed countries.

The Second Limitation: Imbalance with Changing Global Economy

Besides the likelihood of causing global economic and financial imbalance, the current international monetary system also has some other defects, such as the unstable exchange rate system and undeveloped crisis relief or bailout mechanisms. The outbreak of the recent financial crisis not only highlighted internal contradictions and external conflicts since the formulation of the current international monetary system but also significantly changed the global economy.

Emerging economies such as China, Brazil, and South Africa had strong economic growth in the last few years. Total economic aggregates of emerging countries as a percentage of the world's GDP are increasing, and so are their contributions to global economic growth. According to the World Bank and other organizations, as early as 2007, 50 percent of global economic growth was attributed to China, India, and Russia, and the contributions from all emerging economies to global economic growth exceeded 60 percent. Because the international monetary system is backed by national economy and financial strength, the development of emerging economies will lead to corresponding international monetary system adjustments to reflect a new global economic order. It means that as emerging economies continue to grow, their currencies will have a role in the future international monetary system.

On the other hand, as the international economic order changes, especially since the recent financial crisis, emerging economies represented by BRIC have far outgrown developed countries. The proportion of the U.S. economy to the global economy has dropped from more than 50 percent to about 25 percent, and total U.S. imports and exports as a percentage of the global trade volume have dropped from one-sixth to one-tenth. But the U.S. dollar still accounts for two-thirds of global reserves (Table 6.2). Using one-fourth of world economic power to support two-thirds of international reserves is hard for the current international monetary system to sustain.

We can reasonably conclude that as the world economy on which the current international monetary system is based undergoes substantial transformations, emerging economies will inevitably request higher participation and more voting rights during the reconstruction of the international monetary system in order to balance the costs and benefits of global economic development.

Table 6.2 The U.S. Economy and U.S. Dollar During 1947–2008 (percent)

Year	The Proportion of U.S. Economy to the World Economy			The Status of the U.S. Dollar in World Money Markets	
	GDP	Imports	Exports	Percentage of Foreign Exchange Reserves	Percentage of Foreign Exchange Transactions
1947	50.0	—	—	—	—
1965	35.3	15.9	13.4	—	—
1980	25.9	12.0	12.3	—	—
1985	33.7	13.0	175	—	—
1990	25.8	12.6	14.2	—	45
1995	24.7	12.6	14.2	59.0	—
1998	29.4	13.8	16.3	69.3	43.5
1999	30.3	13.8	17.5	71.0	—
2000	30.6	13.7	18.4	71.1	—
2001	32.5	13.3	18.0	71.5	45.15
2002	32.2	12.4	17.5	67.1	—
2003	29.4	11.0	16.4	65.9	—
2004	27.8	10.3	15.8	65.9	44.35
2005	27.4	10.1	15.7	66.9	—
2006	26.9	9.8	15.1	65.5	—
2007	25.2	9.5	13.7	64.1	43.15
2008	23.4	10.7	13.2	64.0	—

Source: Data from Li Ruogu (2009).

International Monetary System Adjustment: From "Multicurrencies with a Dominant One" to "Multicurrencies Balancing"

History shows that a sustainable balance can be achieved only if the international monetary system structure is in basic conformity with the economic strength of a major country. With this consensus, we can conclude that system restructuring essentially depends on the changes in major countries' economic strength.

Although international monetary system reform after the financial crisis is imperative, there will not be many changes to the current dollar standard. The reform will be a long-term, progressive, and incremental process. First, the United States is still the strongest economy in the world. There won't be a solution to the Triffin Dilemma for any single currency attempting to replace the U.S. dollar as the new international reserve currency. Second, the history of the international monetary system tells us that an old system will likely remain in place before a new one takes its place, and most nations are reluctant to see the uncertainties associated with abrupt system changes. Third, the weakening dollar causes huge unrealized losses to the central banks of those countries whose balance sheets carry huge foreign reserves, which also becomes a major barrier to the reform.

In the short term, the current system can be adjusted slightly. For example, special drawing rights (SDRs) can be more widely used, the IMF can be adjusted, and international coordination and cooperation can be enhanced. In terms of adjusting the SDR's pricing components and increasing its supply and usage, Professor Robert Mundell suggested changing the original weighting structure[1] and setting the total weight of the U.S. dollar and the euro at 70 percent and dividing the remaining 30 percent evenly between the Japanese yen, the British pound, and the Chinese yuan.[2] In terms of the reforms of the IMF to increase the fairness and legitimacy of international organizations, it is necessary for the IMF to transfer voting power from developed countries to developing countries through the adjustment of voting rights and encourage the coordination of government policies between developed and developing countries. In terms of enhancing communication and negotiations among all countries, the G-20 consists of major developed and developing countries that should play more important roles in the future.

In the long term, we must thoroughly change the current international monetary system. There are three fundamental choices. The first one is to return to a currency system based on physical commodities instead of the credit-based currency system, that is, returning to either the gold standard or the standard based on certain commodities. The second choice is to create a global central bank and a global currency. The third choice is to diversify reserve currencies or build a new diversified international monetary system. By using currencies based on certain physical commodities, the first choice will obviously fail to meet the needs for currencies in a highly developed economic and trading environment. The second choice to establish a global currency that overrides all sovereignty is a utopian dream.[3] Relatively speaking, a diversified international monetary system in a pluralized world should be a relatively feasible choice. It not only fits current global political and economic situations but also meets the mutual interests of developed and developing nations.

As the international monetary system is transforming toward the balancing of multiple currencies, RMB will undoubtedly play a more important role and become more influential, especially as China becomes one of the largest trading partners in the world. As the global economy continues to grow under current structures for another 30 years, the fifth generation of international monetary system is very likely to emerge, in which the U.S. dollar, the euro, and the Chinese yuan will become equally important (Figure 6.2).

Figure 6.2 International Monetary System Reform

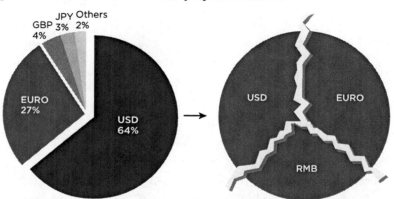

Note: The left graph refers to the proportion of four currencies in international reserves in 2008. The right graph refers to the relationship among three dominant currencies, not their proportion.

Challenges to International Monetary System Reform: "5012" and Currency Integration

It is necessary to point out that the fifth-generation international monetary system is a trend-following idea. Whether the idea will turn into a reality depends on two major challenges. The first challenge is the timing of international currency substitutions, or "5012." The number 5012 refers to the period from 1894, when the United States surpassed Great Britain in terms of GDP, till the end of World War II, when the U.S. dollar replaced the British pound as the international reserve currency. The process took 50 years, witnessing 1 Great Depression and 2 world wars before the final substitution of the international reserve currency and the adjustment of the world economic and political structure.

What 5012 demonstrates is that the rising of a country's currency lags behind the rising of its economy by about half a century. If the year 2040 were set as the target to globalize RMB, the globalization of the Chinese yuan and the rising of the economy would have basically been accomplished at the same time, which is contrary to the assumption of 5012. Whether RMB is able to be the third international currency is still controversial among academics. Ronald McKinnon (2004) was optimistic, believing that RMB could realistically become the third-largest international currency within a short period of time as the Chinese economy continues growing, while Mr. Huang Da, a famous Chinese economist, argued that the rising of the Chinese yuan would be a long and progressive process, and every effort should be made to avoid the "aggressive driving" attitude. The history of the economy indicates that for one economy and its currency to surpass a more powerful one, it would have to use a steady and progressive strategy. Premature surpassing might brew up huge potential financial risks that would be ultimately detrimental to economic development. Therefore, the prospect of globalizing RMB will be bright, but the road may be bumpy.

The other challenge to the globalization of RMB comes from currency integration. The challenge will arise if the dollar, the euro, and the yuan dominate the world monetary system in about 30 years, as we expect today. Then we would have to consider how to deal with fluctuations of exchange rates among these three dominant currencies and how to prevent exchange rate risks. Obviously, without stable exchange rates among these three currencies, the global financial system would not be stable. In this case, would there be a supersovereign currency that integrates global currencies and bypasses sovereignty? There was a famous debate in the 1980s between British Prime Minister Margaret Thatcher, German Chancellor Helmut Schmidt, and French President Valery Giscard d'Estaing. The former insisted on the sovereignty of a nation's currency, and the latter two insisted on the feasibility and necessity of having a single currency (Figure 6.3).

Based on the optimum currency area theory, currency integration requires that currency union members not only allow factors of production to flow freely between each other but also have more or less the same economic development level, highly integrated trade and finance, and similar historical and cultural backgrounds. Currently, even in the Euro zone where a single currency is circulating, each member's fiscal policy and bond market varies and the gaps in economic development are widening, taking the Euro zone on a bumpy ride to economic development. The Greek debt crisis in 2010 revealed to some extent the problem in the European Union. Compared to

Figure 6.3 The Debate on Currency Integration

Pro: Prime Minister Thatcher

Opinion: Currency is a symbol of sovereignty, so she insists on "one country, one currency."

Result: Britain joins EU but not Euro zone.

Con: Chancellor Schmidt and President d'Estaing

Opinion: Currency is related to the economy and market. A single currency can exist in a market in which factors of production flow freely in certain areas, so they insist on "one market, one currency."

Result: Euro was created centering on Germany and France.

Europe, Asian political and economic situations are more complicated. There are huge differences in economic development and values. It would be very difficult to have an Asian yuan. A single global currency would be even more difficult.

Marching Toward the World: The Present and Future of RMB

Political polarization and economic globalization are two features of the world nowadays. A diversified international monetary system featured by multicurrencies with a dominant one will be the direction of future international monetary system reform. After the worst financial crisis during the last almost 100 years, the result of the war between the "existing hegemony" and "emerging forces" will ultimately determine the new international monetary pattern.

Are traditional major countries able to maintain their international positions? Can emerging countries win enough voting power in the international monetary competition? As a representative of emerging countries, China has maintained stable economic growth and gradually executed financial opening. Is Chinese currency able to take advantage of the historic opportunity and become a major currency in the international monetary system? This is the focal point among many economists.

Current Status

The internationalization of a currency means the process of a currency reaching beyond its national or regional borders, gradually functioning as a medium of exchange, a measure of value, and a means of storage and eventually becoming an international currency. Concerning the definition of an international currency, Cohen (1971) defined it this way: From the perspective of currency functions, an international currency is one universally accepted and used in global markets, fully or partially performing the functions of the pricing unit for international settlement, means of circulation, payment, and reserves. From the perspective of the usage scope, an international currency is not only used within a certain country but also used as investment in certain international communities or the whole world. Based on this definition, Hartmann (1988) looked at different functions of an international currency from the official sector and private sector (Table 6.3).

Under the gold standard, gold was an international currency and a valuable commodity itself. It was freely convertible and circulating worldwide and spontaneously regulated the volume of currency in circulation. But in the age of credit-based currency, as political and economic power of a country changes, it is rather difficult for a country's currency, except a few such as the British pound and the U.S. dollar, to assume all six major functions mentioned above. Generally speaking, if a currency is able to perform some of these six functions in the world, it can be considered an international currency.

The globalization of a currency is a dynamic process, and the globalization progress of each country's currency as well as its result will also vary. In terms of currency circulation areas, the globalization of

Table 6.3 Classification of International Currency Functions

	Official Sectors	**Private Sectors**
Measurement of Value	Determine the exchange rate parity and function as an "anchor" for floating exchange rates	Serve as a pricing unit in trade and financial transactions
Medium of Exchange	Intervene in the foreign exchange market so as to achieve the balance of international payments	Serve as the medium of exchange directly or indirectly for exchange of currencies in commodity trade and capital transactions
Means of Storage	Use international currency itself and other financial assets valued by the international currency as reserve assets	Serve as a currency for private investment in financial assets

a currency can be viewed from three levels, peripheral, regional, and global. In terms of functions, a currency can be used as a means of circulation, payment, or storage. Among these functions, the most important one is value storage. If a currency has been used for international reserves, it can be considered an international currency. Partial globalization refers to the limited number of functions that a currency performs in the global economy, usually one or two in the above-mentioned categories.

Currently, RMB has crossed the national borders and performed these six major functions in neighboring countries and regions to some extent. It has not yet become a true international currency. As the Chinese economy continues to grow and China is more involved in the international monetary system, the globalization of RMB will become a long-term trend. Especially after the recent global financial crisis, there are signs that the speed has picked up.

Looking at currency functions for the official sectors, we see that China actively participated in the East Asian area currency cooperation and set up a flexible mutual assistance mechanism. China took part in bilateral currency swaps as suggested in the Chiang Mai Initiative and signed bilateral swap agreements with Thailand, Japan, South Korea, Malaysia, the Philippines, and Indonesia with total value of US$23.5 billion. As the Chiang Mai Initiative gradually shifted from bilateral to multilateral agreements, China was actively involved in providing funding for regional foreign exchange reserves to improve the regional multilateral financial assistance mechanism. In December 2009 China signed a multilateral agreement to provide 32 percent of the total US$120 billion funding, equivalent to Japan's share. Since 2008 the People's Bank of China has signed eight bilateral currency swap agreements with the central bank or monetary authority of South Korea, Hong Kong, Malaysia, Belarus, Indonesia, Argentina, Iceland, and Singapore, totaling 803.5 billion yuan (Table 6.4). In December 2006, for the first time, RMB was designated as a reserve currency by the Philippines, and the central banks of Malaysia, South Korea, and Cambodia later followed suit.

Table 6.4 Bilateral Currency Swap Agreements Between China and Other Countries and Regions (100 millions of yuan)

Participants	Amount	Time of Signing
China—South Korea	1,800	December 2008
Mainland China—Hong Kong	2,000	January 2009
China—Malaysia	800	February 2009
China—Belarus	200	March 2009
China—Indonesia	1,000	March 2009
China—Argentina	700	March 2009
China—Ireland	35	June 2010
China—Singapore	1,500	July 2010
Total	8,035	

In terms of the private sectors, tourism and international trade promoted RMB circulation and usage in surrounding countries or regions. In 2004 mainland China signed an agreement with Hong Kong and Macao, the Closer Economic Partnership Arrangement (CEPA), and in 2010 an agreement with Taiwan, the Economic Cooperation Framework Agreement (ECFA). As a result, RMB circulation and usage in Hong Kong, Macao, and Taiwan has reached a significant level. With more trade and large number of tourists, the circulation of RMB in other neighboring countries or regions has also grown continuously. Especially during the first half of 2010, the trade volume between China and ASEAN countries jumped 54.7 percent and the circulation of RMB in the ASEAN areas increased significantly, thanks to the opening of the China-ASEAN Free Trade Area.

In terms of cross-border trade denominated in RMB, China issued the Announcement on the Pilot Program for Increasing Cross Border Trade Settlement in RMB in July 2009, signaling the official kickoff of settling cross-border trade in RMB. In June 2010 the pilot program was extended to 20 provinces and cities inside China and became applicable to offshore settlement with every country and region. The pilot program covers commodity trade, services, and other current account transactions.

As cross-border trade is settled in RMB, the purchases and sales of RMB in the international market are also becoming more active. Non-Deliverable Forward (NDF) transactions against RMB grow rapidly, and the total NDF trade volume has far exceeded the foreign exchange volume traded in the domestic market. More Chinese financial institutions or foreign enterprises start to issue bonds denominated in RMB in foreign financial markets. For example, Chinese financial institutions issued bonds denominated in RMB in Hong Kong. Foreign financial organizations issued bonds denominated in RMB in the Chinese financial market.

The Potential Path for RMB Globalization: A Three-Step Strategy

Generally speaking, the internationalization of a currency requires strong support from economic strength, a united and stable political environment, a large volume of international trade, a robust financial market, and stable internal and external asset valuation.

Looking at the history of the GBP, USD, DEM, and JPY, we know that the internationalization of a currency usually takes three stages. The first stage sees the rise of a currency from a domestic means of payments and transactions to one used in the settlement of regional or international trade. The second stage features the rise of the currency from mainly for trade settlement to use for financial transactions and pricing international commodities. The last stage is characterized by the rise of the currency from financial transactions to use for international reserves. The British pound and the U.S. dollar took 55 and 50 years respectively to become major international reserve currencies.

Accordingly, the internationalization of RMB will also be a progressive and long-term process. China should apply a strategy that will take three steps, each with two targets, to accomplish the internationalization of RMB in the coming 30 years (Figure 6.4).

Concerning the scope of RMB, the target for the first 10-year period is the acceptance of RMB by neighboring countries and regions.

Figure 6.4 The Three-Step Strategy for the Internationalization of RMB

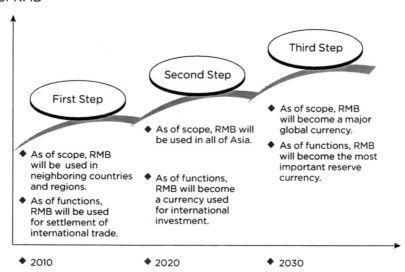

First Step

◆ As of scope, RMB will be used in neighboring countries and regions.

◆ As of functions, RMB will be used for settlement of international trade.

Second Step

◆ As of scope, RMB will be used in all of Asia.

◆ As of functions, RMB will become a currency used for international investment.

Third Step

◆ As of scope, RMB will become a major global currency.

◆ As of functions, RMB will become the most important reserve currency.

◆ 2010   ◆ 2020   ◆ 2030

Note: The period for each step is approximately 10 years. Actual timing will not be as exact as shown and will need to be adjusted according to the situation.

The target for the second 10-year period is the acceptance of RMB by all of Asia. The target for the last 10-year period is the acceptance of RMB in the world and the status of an international reserve currency. Concerning the functions of RMB, the target for the first step is to promote RMB in international trade settlement. The target for the second step is to use RMB in international investment. The target for the last step is to use RMB as one of the international reserve currencies.

Searching for a law from history does not necessarily mean we try to repeat history. The current international currency system is facing unprecedented gaps and imbalance between developed and developing countries, as well as the first structural changes between the oriental and occidental civilizations. It is a long-term war between the old system and the new system during the rise of RMB as an international currency.

Current conditions and progress indicate that the internationalization of RMB has begun. RMB has begun to partially perform the functions of an international currency in neighboring countries and regions. However, there are restrictions from the macroeconomic and microeconomic environment that hinder the process. Meanwhile, the internationalization of RMB will weaken the effectiveness of Chinese monetary policies, reduce the independence of the domestic economy, and increase exchange rate volatility. These issues will need to be addressed during the process.

Managing RMB and Multiple Currencies

It is necessary to point out that an international monetary system under which one super economic power supplies the global currency has maintained relative exchange rate stability and generated global economic growth during a certain period in history. Since the end of the twentieth century, emerging markets have gradually grown and the global economy has changed. The international monetary system dominated by the U.S. dollar is facing changes. The recent financial crisis stemming from the U.S. subprime mortgage crisis once again revealed the defects and systemic risks inherent in the global financial system.

When a nation's currency is used to price commodities and settle international trade as well as serve as international reserves, it can promote economic globalization, but eventually it will be harmed by the defects inherent in the monetary system. The return of the Triffin Dilemma is like a dark shadow cast on economic globalization and will constantly test the rationality of the international financial system. As for countries that issue reserve currencies, conflicting objectives never allow them to achieve simultaneous internal and external economic balance, forcing them to painfully choose between inflation and excessive liquidity.

Frankly, the outbreak of the financial crisis once again brought up the issue of international reserve currency. It is becoming more pressing for increasingly closely interconnected global economies to correct the inherent flaws of the current international monetary system and establish an international reserve system that can not only maintain global financial stability but also promote world economic development. In terms of future reform, the old system dominated by the U.S. dollar will need to be gradually changed. Major global economies will need to share the responsibility of maintaining the stability of the global monetary system. This will eventually lead to a new diversified monetary system composed of the U.S. dollar, the euro, the British pound, RMB, and the Japanese yen, which will facilitate the stability of the global financial system and maintain sustainable world economic growth.

Undoubtedly, as the global economy is transforming from unilateralism to multilateralism, the international monetary system will also transform from one dominated by a single currency to one where multiple currencies harmoniously coexist. In the process of rebuilding the international monetary system, as a large developing country and the fastest-growing emerging economy in the world, China should enable RMB to play a more active and constructive role in the future monetary framework under which multiple currencies will share global management responsibilities.

NOTES

Chapter 2

1. Whether a country is considered innovation oriented depends on whether its economic growth driver is labor and capital or science and technology. In this regard, developed countries and developing countries conform to the law of 7—3—3—7, which says that 70 percent of a developed country's economic growth is driven by science and technology and 30 percent by labor and capital, whereas in a developing country, science and technology drive 30 percent while capital, labor, and raw materials drive 70 percent.

Chapter 4

1. Although CPI is used internationally, it includes the prices of goods that are not traded. Alternative indexes, such as PPI, GDP deflator, unit labor cost, and so on, are not widely accepted.
2. Compared with easily accessible and real-time exchange rate data, CPI and PPI generally lag behind by one month, GDP deflator by at least a quarter, and unit labor cost by an even longer period. What's more, the statistical definitions of different countries vary significantly, and some countries may not even have comparable data.
3. As the IMF focuses on calculating the RER (real exchange rate), the RER is often used to calculate the RMB exchange rate. Generally speaking, the PPP model or extended PPP model assumes that the PPP theory is effective in the long run, that the relationships among macroeconomic variables are stable, and that the long-term exchange rate will settle at a level determined by PPP despite short-term deviations due to external factors. The PPP model is the most widely used because it does not need many inputs and researchers can select variables based on their own judgments. The IMF issues exchange rates based on the International Notice System (INS) that came into being in 1983 to supervise the exchange rates of its members. INS is not an exchange rate but an index of exchange rates. According to the INS definition, IMF members calculate the exchange rate index by three methods. Unit Labor Cost Based REER (real effective exchange rate) is used in 21 industrialized countries where labor costs are easily accessible. Consumer Price Index

REER is used by original member countries, including 21 industrialized countries and emerging markets that mainly export manufactured products. The third method is used by new IMF members that joined in the 1990s, such as China, which uses import and export commodities as weights to calculate the exchange rate index.

Chapter 6

1. The original weights are 44 percent of USD, 34 percent of EUR, 11 percent of JPY, and 11 percent of GBP.
2. The supply of SDRs will need to be increased to match the global GDP. In terms of usage, SDRs should not be limited to governments and can be gradually accessible by private users. Specifically, the proposal includes opening the SDR account to private sectors, developing financial tools priced in SDRs and a financial market using these tools, and designing an SDR settlement system.
3. This choice cannot be realized. In 1860 Great Britain rejected the proposal from France to establish a single global currency. In 1944 the United States rejected the proposal of a global currency from Great Britain.

BIBLIOGRAPHY

Bhagwati, Jagdish. *A Stream of Windows: Unsettling Reflections on Trade, Immigration and Democracy*. Cambridge: MIT Press, 1998.

Chen Yulu. 陈雨露，2008：人民币均衡汇率：理论溯源与汇率的政治经济学视角，《货币金融评论》11期.

Cohen, Benjamin J. *The Future of Sterling as an International Currency*. London: Macmillan, 1971.

Cohen, Benjamin J. "The Seigniorage Gain of an International Currency: An Empirical Test." *Quarterly Journal of Economics* 85, no. 3 (1971): 494–507.

Federal Reserve Bulletin. Statistical Supplement to the Federal Reserve Bulletin. 1984–2004.

Frankel, J. A. *No Single Currency Regime Is Right for All Countries or at All Times*. Princeton Studies in International Finance, 1999: 215.

Gourinchas, Pierre-Olivier, and Helene Rey. "From World Banker to World Venture Capitalist: US External Adjustment and the Exorbitant Privilege." NBER Working Paper No. 11563 (2005).

Hartmann, Philipp. *Currency Competition and Foreign Exchange Markets: The Dollar, the Yen, and the Euro*. Cambridge, U.K.: Cambridge University Press, 1998.

Hartmann, Philipp. "The International Role of the Euro." *Journal of Policy Modeling* 24 (2002): 315.

Hausmann, Ricardo, Ugo Panizza, and Ernesto Stein. "Why Do Countries Float the Way They Float?" *Journal of Development Economics* 66, no. 2 (2001): 387–414.

Hiro Ho and Menzie Chinn. "Notes on the Calculation of the Chinn-Ito Financial Openness Variable." Working Paper (Feb. 28, 2007).

International Monetary Fund. World Economic Outlook Database. October 2008, http://www.imf.org/external/.

International Monetary Fund. Annual Report, 2007, http://www.imf.org/external/.

International Monetary Fund. Annual Report, 2006, http://www.imf.org/external/.

International Monetary Fund. *Financial Stress and Deleveraging Macrofinancial Implications and Policy*. Global Financial Stability Report. 2008.

International Monetary Fund. International Financial Statistics, 1981–2003, http://www.imf.org/external/.

Krugman, Paul. "The Eternal Triangle." http://web.mit.edu/Krugman/ (1998).

Krugman, Paul. "Vehicle Currencies and the Structure of International Exchange." *Journal of Money, Credit and Banking* (1980).

Li Ruogu (2009). 李若谷，2009：国际货币体系改革与人民币国际化，北京：中国金融出版社

Ma Yong and Chen Yulu. 马勇、陈雨露：资本账户开放与系统性金融危机，《当代经济科学》2010年4期.

McKinnon, Ronald I. "China's New Exchange Rate Policy: Will China Follow Japan into a Liquidity Trap." *Singapore Economic Review* 50 (2005): 463–474.

McKinnon, Ronald I. "The International Dollar Standard and Sustainability of the U. S. Current Account Deficit." Brookings Papers on Economic Activity (2001): 227–240.

McKinnon, Ronald I. "Optimum Currency Areas and the European Experience," *Economics of Transition* 10 (2002): 343–364.

Mundell, Robert A. "Capital Mobility and Stabilization Policy Under Fixed and Flexible Exchange Rate." *Canadian Journal of Economics and Political Science* (Nov. 1963).

Mundell, Robert A. 罗伯特·蒙代尔，2003：蒙代尔经济学文集，北京：中国金融出版社.

Mundell, Robert A. "The Monetary Dynamics of International Adjustment under Fixed and Floating Exchange Rate." *Quarterly Journal of Economics* 74 (1960): 227–257.

Mundell, Robert A., and Alexander K. Swoboda (eds.). *Monetary Problems of the International Economy*. Chicago: University of Chicago Press, 1969.

Portes, Richard, and Helene Rey. "The Emergence of the Euro as an International Currency." *Economic Policy* 26, no. 2 (1998): 307–332.

Sandbeck, Dix. "Bretton Woods and the Forgotten Concept of International Seigniorage." *Economic Reform*, 2003.

Stiglitz, Joseph. (Unknown)

Triffin, Robert. *Gold and the Dollar Crisis*. New Haven: Yale University Press, 1960.

INDEX

Note: page numbers followed by f, t, and n indicate figures, tables, and endnotes, respectively.

Annual Report on Exchange Arrangements and Exchange Restrictions (AREAER) (IMF), 114
ASEAN Countries, 30, 145
Asian financial crisis, 79, 85–86, 87f, 89f, 126
Asset price execution mechanism, 69

Balance of international payments, 99–100, 133–134. *See also* capital account opening
Balance of Payments Manual (IMF), 99–100
Bancor, 131
Banking system, 33–34, 35t–36t, 52–53. *See also* People's Bank of China
Bao-jia administrative system, 15
Beijing Consensus, 31–32
Benchmark interest rate, 65
Bhagwati, Jagdis, 121
Bid price, 76
Big-headed Yuan coin, 19
Bilateral currency swaps, 144–145
Book of Han, 7
Bretton Woods system, 130–131, 132
British pound, 78f, 129–130, 138
Buddhist monasteries, credit from, 8

CAFTA (China-ASEAN Free Trade Area), 30, 145
Capital account opening
  advantages and disadvantages of, 102–103

balance of international payments and the capital account, 99–100
capital transfers and the financial account, 100–101
currency substitution and, 103
foreign exchange certificates and, 109
history and process of, 107–110, 111t–112t
IMF classification and categories of, 114, 115t, 116t–120t, 121
as irreversible trend, 101–102
order and principles for, 123–124
progressive vs. radical approach and financial crises arising from, 104–107, 108t, 121
QFII and WDII system, 110–113
tight vs. loose, 114
timetable for, 122
Capital transfers, 100
Central bank securities, 64–65
Central planning system and monetary policy, 48, 49t, 52
CEPA (Closer Economic Partnership Arrangement), 145
Chenery, Hollis, 37
Chiang Mai Initiative, 144
China-ASEAN Free Trade Area (CAFTA), 30, 145
China Foreign Exchange Trade System, 82
Chinese as a foreign language, 32
Chinese Doctrine of the Mean, viii
Chomsky, Noam, 32
Chu state, 5
Closer Economic Partnership Arrangement (CEPA), 145
Cohen, Benjamin J., 142

Coinage, history of. *See* monetary culture of China, history of

Common monetary policy instruments, 60–61

Conditional restriction principle for capital account opening, 124

Consumer price index (CPI), 56, 151nn1–2

Consumer Price Index REER, 151n3

Controllability, 58, 93

Convertibility of RMB. *See* capital account opening; current account

Copper shells (coins), 3, 5

Cowrie shells, 1–3

CPI (consumer price index), 56, 151nn1–2

Credit
  differential, 53
  in Han dynasty, 7, 8
  in Sui and Tang dynasties, 11
  in Tang dynasty, 10
  Wang Anshi's reform (Yuan), 14–15

Credit-based currency system, 139, 143

Credit execution mechanism, 66

Credit plan system, 51–54

Cross-border trade denominated in RMB, 145–146

Cultural prosperity, 32

Currency. *See also entries at RMB*
  bilateral currency swaps, 144–145
  central planning and, 52
  global, 139, 152n3
  globalization process for, 143–144
  international, defined, 142–143
  international monetary system and global currencies, 125
  strong currencies, 126, 127t

Currency, history of. *See* monetary culture of China, history of

Currency integration, 140–142

Currency stability as monetary policy objective, 56, 71

Currency substitution, 103

Current account
  balance of international payments and, 99, 134
  convertibility and, 69, 90, 92, 109, 122
  exchange rate and, 75, 88
  exchange restrictions, removal of, 110
  financial firewall and, 34
  international monetary system and, 122
  monetary policy and, 61

Deng Xiaoping, 54

Deposit reserve ratio, 62t, 64, 65

Differential credit, 53

Direct credit control instruments, 61

Direct investment, 101

Direct regulation and control in monetary policy, 48, 68

Disaster relief credit, in Han dynasty, 7–8

Discounting, 62t

Dollar, U.S.
  Bretton Woods system and, 130–131
  currencies pegged to, 85, 86, 132, 135
  gold standard and, 126
  in international monetary system, 129–130
  limits of the dollar standard system, 133–136
  RMB exchange rates against, 78f, 89f
  status of, in world markets(1947–2008), 137t
  tael replaced with, 20
  Triffin Dilemma, 131–132, 133, 138, 148

Double circulation of physical resources and financial capital, 133–134

Eastern Europe, 31

Economic Cooperation Framework Agreement (ECFA), 145

Economic development stages, 27–28

Economic growth, Chinese. *See also* growth without crisis
  exchange rate and, 77–79

GDP growth and GDP per capita,
    25–26, 28
inflation rate and, 53–54
as monetary policy objective, 57, 71
Emerging economies, growth in, 136
Employment, full, 55
Equilibrium exchange rate of RMB,
    81–83
Euro, 78f, 141
Exchange rates. *See also* RMB
    exchange rate
floating, 63t, 126, 129, 131
foreign exchange rate, defined, 75
international monetary system and,
    125
managed floating exchange rate
    system, 83, 85, 87–90
as monetary policy instrument, 63t
Exchange rate stability, 55, 61–63
Exchange shops, 17–19
Exports. *See* trade, foreign

Fabi, 20
Feiqian ("money on the fly"), 10, 24
Fen, 22
"5012," 140
Financial, globalization, 101
Financial account, 101
Financial crises from capital account
    opening, 104–107, 108t. *See also*
    global financial crisis; growth
    without crisis
Financial firewall, 34
Financial freedom, 43–44
Financial strategy for growth without
    crisis, 41–44
Flexibility, 95
Foreign exchange
monetary policy and inflows of,
    62–64
supply and demand of, 76, 88, 90
Foreign exchange certificates, 109
Foreign exchange rate. *See* exchange
    rates; RMB exchange rate
Foreign exchange reserves, vii, 20, 33
Foreign investment, vii, 27–28, 110,
    111t, 112t

Foreign trade, 28–30, 146
Forward exchange rate, 76
Freedom, financial, 43–44
French franc, 129–130
Friedman, Milton, 25
Full employment, 55

G-20 (Group of 20), 138
GDP (gross domestic product)
aggregate and growth rate, 57f
growth rate in, 25–26, 28, 57
per capita, 25–26, 28
predictions on, 40–41
GDP deflator, 151nn1–2
Genoa Conference (1922), 129
Global currency, 139, 152n3
Global financial crisis, vii, 42, 43–44,
    148–149
Global financial system, restructuring
    of, 43
Globalization, financial, 101
Globalization of currencies. *See*
    international monetary system
    (IMS)
Global thinking pattern, viii
Goal-oriented principle for capital
    account opening, 123–124
Gold currency, 5
Gold standard
international currency and, 143
international monetary system and,
    126, 129
Song dynasty and, 13
Yuan dynasty and, 14
Gold transaction standard, 19
Gold yuan banknote, 20
Green seedling act, 14–15
Gross domestic product. *See* GDP
Growth without crisis
Chinese model and Beijing Consensus,
    30–32
cultural prosperity and, 32
economic foundation for, 33–40
financial strategy for, 41–44
foreign trade growth, 28–30
GDP growth and GDP per capita,
    25–26, 28

Chinese model and Beijing Consensus
(*Cont.*):
industrial economy strategy for,
44–46
meaning of, 25
predictions of growth, 40–41
stages of economic development and,
27–28

Han dynasty, 6–8
Han Fei, 4
Hartmann, Philipp, 143
Hong Xiuquan, 18
Huang Da, 140
Hu Hai, Emperor, 6
Huizong Emperor (Zhao Ji), 11–12

ICBC (Industrial and Commercial
Bank of China), 34
IMF. *See* International Monetary Fund
Imports. *See* trade, foreign
Impossible Trinity theory, 103
Independence, 92–93
Indirect credit control instruments,
61
Indirect regulation and control in
monetary policy, 48–49, 60, 68
Industrial and Commercial Bank of
China (ICBC), 34
Industrial economy strategy, 44–46
Industrialization stage, 37–38
Industrial restructuring, 44–45
Inflation and monetary policy, 49–50,
56
Inflation rate and growth rate, 53–54
Innovation-oriented development, 46,
151n1 (ch2)
INS (International Notice System),
151n3
Instructive credit plans, 62t
Interbank market, 61
Interest rate execution mechanism, 66,
68–69
Interest rates, 63t, 65
International currency, defined,
142–143
International Monetary Fund (IMF)
Articles of Agreement, 110

Balance of Payments Manual,
99–100
capital account transaction
categories, 114, 115t, 116t–120t
real exchange rate (RER) and, 151n3
reforms to, 138
White Plan and, 130–131
International monetary system (IMS)
defined, 128
dollar standard system, limits of,
133–136
historical stages and currency
substitutions, 128–133
RMB globalization, challenges to,
140–142
RMB globalization, current status
of, 142–146
RMB globalization, potential path
for, 146–148
strong economies and strong
currencies and, 125–126, 127t
unilateral-to-multilateral structural
reform, 126–128, 137–142, 149
International Notice System (INS),
151n3

Jamaica system, 131
Japanese yen, 78f, 138
Jianwen Emperor (Zhu Yunwen), 16
jiao, 22
jiaozi ("voucher for exchange"), 12, 24
Jin dukedom, 3–4
Jing Emperor (Liu Qi), 7
Jingzhou, 5

Kangxi Emperor, 17
Keynes, John Maynard, 131
Keynesian school, 55
Keynes Plan, 131
Kublai Khan, 13–14

Latin America, 27, 31, 104
Law of the People's Bank of China,
54–55, 61, 71
Legalist school of thought, 4
Lei Lutai, 17–18
Li Longji, Emperor Xuanzong, 9
Li Shimin, Emperor Taizhong, 8–9, 11

Liu Bang, Emperor, 6
Liu Che, Emperor Wu, 6–7
Liu Qi, Emperor Jing, 7
Li Yuan, 8, 11
Lu state, 4

Macroeconomic management system, 48, 49t
Managed floating exchange rate system, 83, 85, 87–90, 135
Market economy, socialist, 27–28, 84, 91
Market transaction law, 15
Ma Yinchu, 20
McKinnon, Ronald, 140
Microeconomy and monetary policy instruments, 72
Mingcheng Emperor (Zhu Di), 16
Ming dynasty, 16–17
Monetary culture of China, history of demarcation between world civilizations and evolution of Chinese money, 22–24
    Han dynasty, 6–8
    Ming dynasty, 16–17
    North China People's Government and the Renminbi, 21–22
    Qin dynasty, 5–6
    Qing dynasty, 17–19
    Republic of China, 19–20
    Shang and Zhou dynasties, 1–5
    Song dynasty, 11–13, 14
    Sui dynasty, 8, 11
    Tang dynasty, 8–11
    Yuan dynasty, 13–15
Monetary policy
    credit plan system, 51–54
    evolution of, 48–51
    execution mechanism, 65–70
    future of, 70–73
    goals and objectives, 54–57
    intermediate target of, 57–60
    meaning and purpose of, 47
    objectives evolution for major developing countries, 59t
    People's Bank of China as central bank, 47–48
    policy instruments, 60–65

Monetary system, international. See international monetary system (IMS)
Money shops, 10–11, 17, 20
"Money-snatching officials," 11
Money supply
    credit plan and, 52
    goals for, 54
    monetary policy and, 58–60, 62–64
Monitoring, 42, 96
Multicurrencies balancing, 137–142
Multicurrencies with a dominant one, 132, 137–142
Mundell, Robert, 126, 138

Natural resources, 45–46
NDF (Non-Deliverable Forward) transactions, 146
Nixon, Richard, 126
Nominal effective exchange rate, 56, 75–76
Non-Deliverable Forward (NDF) transactions, 146
North China People's Government, 21–22

Offer price, 76
On Coins (Zhang Jiuling), 9–10
Open market operations instrument, 62t
Optimum currency area theory, 141
Optional monetary policy instruments, 61

Paper currency
    fabi, 20
    feiqian ("money on the fly"), 10, 24
    jiaozi ("voucher for exchange"), 12, 24
    negotiable paper for salt-transactions, 12–13, 24
    "of the Great Ming," 16
    Zhongtong-reign Currency, 14
People's Bank of China
    bilateral currency swaps, 144
    central bank designation, 48
    credit plan and, 52–53
    exchange rate and, 76, 80, 81, 86, 92

People's Bank of China (*Cont.*):
  formation of, 47
  monetary policy and, 54–55
  RMB administration by, 21–22
Pilot Program for Increasing Cross
    Border Trade Settlement,
    145–146
Planned economy. *See* central planning
    system and monetary policy
Portfolio investment, 101
PPI (producer price index), 56,
    151nn1–2
PPP (purchasing power parity) model,
    81, 151n3
Predictability, in monetary policy, 58
Price-based monetary policy
    instruments, 71–72
Price stability and monetary policy, 55,
    61–63
Producer price index (PPI), 56,
    151nn1–2
Progressiveness, 92, 93, 95–96
Purchasing power parity (PPP) model,
    81, 151n3

Qin dynasty, 5–6
Qing dynasty, 17–19
Qi state, 4
Qualified Domestic Institutional
    Investors (QDII), 110–113
Qualified Foreign Institutional
    Investors (QFII), 110–113

Ramo, Joshua Cooper, 32
Real effective exchange rate (REER),
    75–76, 151n3
Real exchange rate (RER), 151n3
REER (real effective exchange rate),
    75–76, 151n3
Regional economic development,
    strategy for, 45–46
Regional multilateral financial
    assistance, 144
Relending, 62t
Relevance, in monetary policy, 58
Renminbi. *See* RMB
Renzong Emperor (Zhao Zhen), 14
Republic of China, currency in, 19–20

RER (real exchange rate), 151n3
Reserve assets, 101
Retail credit plans, 52
Risk control principle for capital
    account opening, 123
RMB (Renminbi)
  creation of, 21
  cross-border trade denominated in
    RMB, 145–146
  series of, 21–22
  units and fractional units of, 22
  value stability, 71
RMB convertibility. *See* capital
    account opening; current account
RMB effective exchange rate, 56
RMB exchange rate
  defined, 76
  economy, influences on, 77–80
  equilibrium exchange rate, 81–83
  fixed vs. floating, 76
  foreign exchange rate, defined, 75
  history of system of, 84–90
  monetary policy and, 60
  nominal effective vs. real effective,
    75–76
  quotes and forward transactions,
    76–77
  reform directions, 94–96
  reform objectives, 91
  reform principles, 91–93
  SAFE and administration of, 80–81
  against USD, 89f
  against USD, GBP, EURO, and JPY,
    78f
RMB globalization
  balancing of multiple currencies and,
    139
  currency integration as challenge to,
    140–142
  current status of, 142–146
  5012 as challenge to, 140
  potential path for, 146–148
Roach, Stephen, 30

SAFE (State Administration of Foreign
    Exchange), 80–81, 82
Salt-transaction negotiable paper,
    12–13, 24

Sang Hongyang, 23
Savings deposits in Tang dynasty, 10–11
Savings rate, 34, 36f
Science and technology, 46
SDRs (special drawing rights), 138, 152n1
Shaanxi jiaozi currency, 12
Shang and Zhou dynasties, 1–5
Shang Yang, 4
Shen Buhai, 4
Shenzong Emperor (Zhao Xu), 14
Shunzhi, Emperor, 16–17
Silver ingots, 13, 16, 17
Silver purity, 17
Silver standard, 13, 19
Sima Guang, 15
Sima Qian, 22–23
Single whip taxation, 16
Socialist market economy, 27–28, 84, 91
Song dynasty, 11–13, 14
Southeast Asia, 104. See also CAFTA
Special drawing rights (SDRs), 138, 152n1
State Administration of Foreign Exchange (SAFE), 80–81, 82
Stiglitz, Joseph, 135
Sui dynasty, 8, 11
Sun Yat-sen, 19
Supply and demand of foreign exchange, 76, 88, 90

Taizhong Emperor (Li Shimin), 8–9, 11
Tang dynasty, 8–11
Taxation, 10, 16
Three Highs and One Low enterprises, 45
Trade, foreign, 28–30, 146
Triffin, Robert, 132
Triffin Dilemma (or Paradox), 131–132, 133, 138, 148

Unita, 130
United States. See dollar, U.S.; U.S. economy in proportion to world economy

Unit labor cost, 151nn1–2
Unit Labor Cost Based REER, 151n3
Urbanization, 38–39
Urban-rural imbalances, 36, 45–46
U.S. economy in proportion to world economy, 137t
Usury, 11

Wang Anshi, 14
Wang Anshi's reform, 14–15
Wang Mang, 7
Washington Consensus, 31–32
Wen Emperor (Yang Jian), 8
White, Harry Dexter, 130
White Plan, 130–131
Window guidance, 62t
World civilizations, demarcation between, 22–24
Wu Emperor (Liu Che), 6–7

Xuanzong Emperor (Li Longji), 9

Yang Jian, Emperor Wen, 8
Yangli, 20
Yeomen money, 11
Ye Shi, 23
Ying Zheng, Emperor, 5–6, 8
Yuan, 5, 22, 138, 140
Yuanbao (silver ingots), 13
Yuan dynasty, 13–15
Yuan Shikai, 19

Zhang Jiuling, 9–10
Zhang Juzheng, 16
Zhao Ji, Emperor Huizong, 11–12
Zhao Xu, Emperor Shenzong, 14
Zhao Zhen, Emperor Renzong, 14
Zhenzong Emperor, 12
Zhongtong-reign Currency, 14
Zhu Di, Emperor Mingcheng, 16
Zhu Yuanzhang, Hongwu Emperor, 16
Zhu Yunwen, Emperor Jianwen, 16
Ziqian credit (Han dynasty), 7

ABOUT THE AUTHOR

Chen Yulu is a professor of finance, an Eisenhower senior visiting fellow, and a Fulbright senior scholar. He serves as president of Renmin University of China, vice-chairman of the China International Finance Association, deputy secretary general and executive director of the China Society for Finance and Banking, is a deputy to the 12th National People's Congress of China, and a Member of the Monetary Policy Committee of the People's Bank of China. For his outstanding service and accomplishments, Professor Chen is also a winner of the National Prize for Doctoral Dissertation Supervisors and many other national, provincial, and ministerial awards. His major research pursuits include financial theory and policy in world-oriented economies and international capital markets.

CPSIA information can be obtained at www.ICGtesting.com
Printed in the USA
BVOW03s2008201014

371587BV00007B/19/P

9 780071 829908